Poison Panic

For my grandparents: Jack, Amy, Bert and Beryl

'The lowest and vilest alleys in London do not present a more dreadful record of sin than does the smiling and beautiful countryside.'

Sir Arthur Conan Doyle, *The Adventures of Sherlock Holmes*

Poison Panic

Arsenic Deaths in 1840s Essex

Helen Barrell

PEN & SWORD TRUE CRIME

First published in Great Britain in 2016 by
Pen & Sword True Crime
an imprint of
Pen & Sword Books Ltd
47 Church Street
Barnsley
South Yorkshire
S70 2AS

ISBN 978 1 47385 207 5

A CIP catalogue record for this book is available from the British
Library

Typeset in Ehrhardt by
Mac Style Ltd, Bridlington, East Yorkshire
Printed and bound in the UK by CPI Group (UK) Ltd,
Croydon, CRO 4YY

Pen & Sword Books Ltd incorporates the imprints of Pen & Sword
Archaeology, Atlas, Aviation, Battleground, Discovery, Family
History, History, Maritime, Military, Naval, Politics, Railways, Select,
Transport, True Crime, and Fiction, Frontline Books, Leo Cooper,
Praetorian Press, Seaforth Publishing and Wharncliffe.

For a complete list of Pen & Sword titles please contact
PEN & SWORD BOOKS LIMITED
47 Church Street, Barnsley, South Yorkshire, S70 2AS, England
E-mail: enquiries@pen-and-sword.co.uk
Website: www.pen-and-sword.co.uk

Contents

Map of Essex.

Illustrations

Note on Text

The primary sources used for this book are contemporary newspapers, censuses, parish registers, wills, Home Office documents and Old Bailey proceedings. Direct speech has been taken from reports of inquests and trials in newspapers. It should go without saying that the newspapers referred to in this book no longer report on trials in the same way they did in the 1840s. They scrupulously follow press guidelines and the various pieces of legislation that have come into place in the intervening years.

Whilst the aim of this book is not to solve the mysteries of these deaths, the reader is left free to formulate their own theories.

Introduction

The Poison Shop

In a satirical sketch called 'The Poison Shop', published in 1849, *Punch* magazine mocked how easy it was to buy poisons. A widow requests threepence worth of laudanum – all the money she has in the world; she presumably intends to take her own life. A little girl says her mother has sent her for 'as much Arsenic as you can for twopence-halfpenny, to kill rats'. The assistant, named Bottles, says, 'Rats! Eh! Father belong to a burial club?' And following the child are six other customers who want arsenic too. Then a mysterious stranger asks for the strongest poison in the shop; Bottles has many for him to choose from – prussic acid, strychnine, belladonna, digitalis and vitriol. The scene ends with Bottles' aside to the audience: 'Ha! A pretty good morning's work; – and if the undertakers don't get a job or two out of it – and perhaps Jack Ketch too – I shall be astonished rayther.'

British readers in the late 1840s would have well understood the satire – the newspapers of the day were filled with inquests from across the country, where deaths were caused by poison. Trials were reported in detail and the deceased's close relative or friend stood in the shadow of the hangman. Leading articles in *The Times* boomed that something must be done – to tighten up the civil registration of deaths and to regulate the sale of poisons and the running of burial clubs. With their generous payouts intended to cover funeral costs, the burial clubs presented the motive; easily obtained poisons provided the weapon; and loose rules for registering deaths concealed the crime.

The English south-eastern county of Essex loomed large in the public imagination, one of the locations where many arsenic murders had allegedly taken place. Sarah Chesham, Mary May and Hannah Southgate would all stand trial, accused of poisoning with arsenic. Their names were linked in the newspapers, the press claiming they were part of a poisoning ring of women who taught each other how to kill with 'white powder'. Their victims were husbands, sons and brothers, and they were murdered, so the papers said,

FATAL FACILITY; OR, POISONS FOR THE ASKING.

Child. "Please, Mister, will you be so good as to fill this bottle again with Lodnum, and let Mother have another pound and a half of Arsenic for the Rats (!)"

Duly Qualified Chemist. "Certainly, Ma'am. Is there any other article?"

One of many anti-poison satires to appear in *Punch*.

for burial club money or to clear the way for a new man. While mainland Europe in the 1840s was convulsed with revolution, the Essex poisonings crystallised the fear that British society was under threat.

Arsenic, arsenic, everywhere

Although it is naturally occurring, the arsenic bought for mere pence from Victorian chemists and grocers was usually the chemical compound arsenic trioxide. A by-product of the ore refining process, this white, flour-like powder was available in large quantities during the Industrial Revolution in Britain. It had many legitimate uses – glass-makers needed it to remove the green tinge from otherwise clear glass, and it was used in the manufacture of perfectly spherical shot. Farmers used it to control pests, and it was a highly effective fungicide; it was present in sheep dip and was used to steep seeds. Arsenic had medicinal and cosmetic uses too, but perhaps its best-known nineteenth-century use was as a dye called Scheele's Green or 'emerald green'. As a metal, it was popular because it wouldn't fade like vegetable dyes, and so was used for wallpaper (which may have killed Napoleon Bonaparte), clothing, and even in food. This had predictably dreadful results: in Northampton in 1848, two men were found guilty of manslaughter when one man died and many other diners fell ill after eating blancmange that had been coloured with 'emerald green'.

Around many ordinary nineteenth-century homes, arsenic in its white powder form was used to kill rats and mice, which were a problem in the badly maintained cottages of the poor. Shops sold commercial preparations that had arsenic as an ingredient, but some would buy white arsenic neat as it was cheaper. A common method was to spread the poison on a slice of buttered bread and leave it by mouse holes.

The Hungry Forties are well known for the tragedy of the potato blight that caused death and emigration on a huge scale in Ireland and the Scottish Highlands. In mainland Europe, food shortages caused by bad harvests stoked feelings of desperation that led to unrest. Potato blight affected crops elsewhere in Britain, too, and the Corn Laws, keeping the price of grain inflated to protect landowners from cheap imports, meant that food for the ordinary British person was expensive, especially as wages were falling.

Although the Corn Laws were abolished in 1846, wages remained depressed and protecting scanty food by lacing the home with deadly poison was a risk that some families felt worth taking.

The Victorian medicine chest

In small doses, arsenic does not kill at once and has a temporary positive effect on the body; it is still used today to cure leukaemia because it prompts the production of normal blood cells. It acts as a stimulant on the metabolism, and so was used in tonics: from the 1780s it was an ingredient in Fowler's Solution, recommended for neuralgia, syphilis, lumbago, epilepsy and skin disorders; unofficially, it was used as an aphrodisiac. Fowler's was available until the 1950s, when it was discovered that long-term users were developing skin cancer. Arsenic was an ingredient in some soaps because it initially helped the complexion, but when used too often it led to illness. Arsenic was one of several poisons used to induce miscarriages at a time when abortion was illegal – unsurprisingly, this sometimes led to the mother's death.

The Victorian medicine chest contained other poisons. Laudanum had long been used as a painkiller and to subdue crying babies, but it was highly addictive, caused hallucinations and in large quantities was used by suicides. Belladonna, or deadly nightshade, was used in ointment to relieve rheumatic pain, or as a sedative, but too much can lead to convulsions and coma. Hemlock was used as a muscle relaxant, a sedative, and in tonics; highly potent, accidental overdoses were easy, causing respiratory collapse and death. Strychnine was used to cure indigestion and revive patients in cases of heart failure, but a large enough dose leads to a painful death where the muscles spasm and the victim eventually asphyxiates. Sarah Chesham's medicine chest was found to contain several poisonous substances used to treat skin conditions, such as nitrate of mercury and blistering flies (a beetle that contained an irritant, used medicinally to raise blisters).

Home remedies were essential in a society where medical help was not always easy to procure. According to the 1841 census, in a population of nearly 350,000 people spread over 979,000 acres there were only nineteen physicians in the whole of Essex – one per 18,500 people. Physicians were expensive, having trained at medical college, and with only nineteen in the

The adverse effects of taking arsenic medicinally were not unknown at the time, as this image from the 1850s shows.

county might have lived some distance from the patient. Most ordinary people relied on the cheaper surgeons and apothecaries, who trained by apprenticeship.

Surgeons' visits and apothecaries' medicines still had to be paid for, so the poor had to first apply to a churchwarden, in order that the parish would cover the cost. The surgeons were often very busy, with many patients dispersed over a large area, particularly a problem in rural districts, so they weren't always able or inclined to visit a patient at the first sign of illness. Instead, they prescribed medication based on the symptoms reported to them, and the patient's family sometimes had a walk of several miles to return to the sickbed. The time taken to procure medical help was used by prosecutors in poison trials to heap guilt on the accused, but the system then in place presented obstacles that caused unavoidable delays.

Civil registration of births, marriages and deaths began in England and Wales in 1837. The word of a medical man wasn't essential when registering a death, and they were usually only brought in if the death subsequently raised suspicions. If a surgeon hadn't been able to visit a patient before they died and the reported symptoms were severe stomach pain, vomiting and purging (the polite nineteenth-century term for diarrhoea), they would often consider the death to have had a natural cause.

Arsenic – or a stomach bug?

Unless an expert subjected the deceased's viscera to toxicological analysis, cause of death might be considered English or Asiatic cholera. The former is perhaps what we would now call an upset stomach – rarely fatal, it mainly occurred during the summer months, and there would be vomiting and 'purging'. Asiatic cholera is what we know of today as cholera, which kills many thousands of people every year in developing countries and flares up at the scene of natural disasters. Caused by a waterborne bacterium, the purging is intense and death is a result of rapid dehydration.

The confusion between arsenic poisoning and the choleras was contentious, coming up again and again at poison trials. So, in 1848, Henry Letheby, a lecturer in Chemistry at the London Hospital, wrote an article in the *Pharmaceutical Journal* explaining in great detail how to tell the symptoms apart and what to look for in the body's evacuations.

It was certainly timely. The disorder and upheaval in mainland Europe led to the perfect conditions for cholera to thrive and spread west towards

Britain. It is unnerving to read newspaper reports of 1848 about the steady advance of the disease from Asia between outraged editorials about arsenic poisoning conspiracies. It was not, perhaps, poisoners that scared the public and the establishment, so much as the terrifying approach of social disorder and disease, but exaggerated poison crime waves sufficed as a scapegoat. Asiatic cholera had killed over 50,000 people in Britain in 1831, and by 1848 it was clear that it would arrive on these shores again.

Detecting arsenic

Over the centuries, arsenic had become legendary for its use by poisoners – colourless and flavourless, it was easy to feed to victims. From the late 1700s, various tests were developed to identify arsenic in human remains, but until the Marsh test in 1836, none were sensitive enough to detect the small amount that might remain after a poisoning.

One of the earliest uses for the Marsh test to detect a crime was in France in 1840, when Marie-Fortunée Lafarge was convicted of her husband's arsenic murder. Her crime became infamous and emphasised the Continental glamour and danger that poisoning still had from the time of Lucretia Borgia.

Poison secretly administered by a trusting hand was deemed morally more repugnant than a physical attack, even though it was rare, and at the time most spousal murders in Britain – over 90 per cent – were committed by men, who beat or stabbed their wives. This isn't to say that the press didn't protest about violence in the home, and sighed at the casual attitude exhibited by some men towards 'disciplining' their wives, but in Victorian England, the home, managed by women, represented a safe place against the disorder in the streets and further afield, in revolutionary Europe. Female poisoners were a threat to the safe haven of home.

In 1841, the German chemist Hugo Reinsch developed a test that detects the presence of any heavy metal in a sample, including arsenic, and was even more accurate than the Marsh test. Reinsch realised that if the body part or stomach contents were dissolved in hydrochloric acid, then when a copper strip was inserted into the solution, a black mirror would appear on it if metals were present. It was possible to weigh the amount of metallic poison found, and estimate how much had been administered.

Portrait of Madame Lafarge, from a report on her trial, 1840.

Professor Alfred Swaine Taylor, a chemist, was a toxicologist sometimes called 'the father of forensic science'. He was the Professor of Medical Jurisprudence at Guy's Hospital in London for forty-six years. Again and again, he would welcome provincial surgeons or their assistants to his

Professor Alfred Swaine Taylor (on the left) performs the Reinsch test with a colleague.

laboratory, where they would deliver jars of digestive organs removed from the cadavers of suspected poison victims. It was up to Professor Taylor to identify any poison in the viscera he was presented with; he set to work with his acids and copper strips, dissolving slivers of stomach and slices of intestine, pouring out stomach contents, looking for that telltale black mirror.

His expertise went beyond identifying the presence of poisons – he could identify blood on pieces of clothing, telling it apart from other stains. He gave evidence at famous nineteenth-century trials, such as that of William Palmer, 'the Rugeley Poisoner', and Franz Müller, who was convicted of the first murder on a British train. Professor Taylor wrote widely, editing the *Medical Gazette* and publishing textbooks on medical jurisprudence, the umbrella term under which forensic science sits. As expert witness, he would attend inquests in country pubs, and trials in county halls and at the Old Bailey, and was frequently the bugbear of county ratepayers who objected to his fees. Away from the grim world of violent death, Professor Taylor had an artistic side: he put his chemical knowledge to use aiding that new invention, photography.

It was Professor Taylor who searched the bodies of the Essex poison panic victims for their hidden secrets. Were they killed with arsenic? Could the tender hand of the dutiful wife, mother or sister also be the hand of a cold-blooded murderer?

Chapter 1

'My mother has been a good mother to we'

Clavering, a village in the far north-west of Essex, is a chocolate box vision of rural England with flower-decked thatched cottages, surrounded by rolling hills. But when the Chesham family lived there in the 1840s, the village suffered from the economic recession that affected the whole of Europe. In East Anglia, wages had fallen and arson of hayricks and farmers' property was not unusual; even women and children fought farmers who denied them the right to glean in the fields. In 1844, someone signing themselves 'Humanitas' wrote to *The Times* from Essex protesting against a petition emanating from the county that demanded that arson should be a capital offence. 'Humanitas' said that rural arson was down to the starvation wages of agricultural labourers, who hoped for the sentence of transportation in the belief that they would be 'worked more easily in a foreign land.'

In 1850, the *Morning Chronicle* published a letter about the poor of Essex, duly reprinted by the *Chelmsford Chronicle:* 'Along the whole line of the country from Castle Hedingham to Clavering, there is an almost continuous succession of bad cottages. Amongst the worse of these might be mentioned in the neighbourhood of Sible Hedingham, Weathersfield, Bardfield, Wicken, and Clavering.' The overcrowded cottages were damp, with grass-covered thatches; the windows were small and admitted little light. It is in just such a dwelling that the Cheshams would have lived.

They were a fairly ordinary family, agricultural labourers who worked for local farmers. Sarah and her husband, Richard, had both been born in Clavering, and in June 1828 they were married in the parish church where they had both been baptised as infants. It was just before Sarah's nineteenth birthday and she was newly pregnant with their first child. They both marked the register, rather than signing their names, which indicates their level of education. Their first child, Harriet, was born in early 1829. There followed

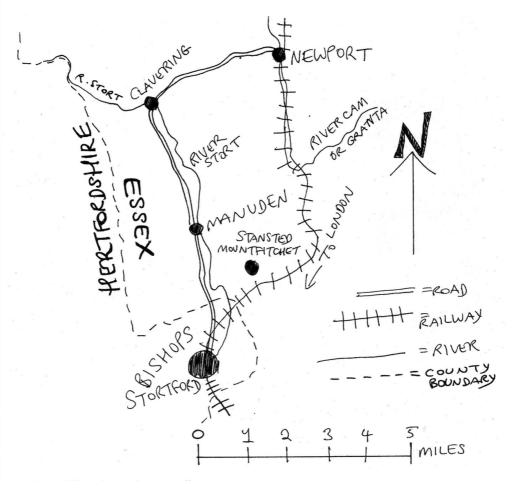

Map of Clavering and surrounding area.

five sons: Philip in about 1831, John in 1832, Joseph in about 1834, James in about 1836, and George in 1839. The Cheshams were luckier than other families of the same period – none of their children died in early childhood, even though infant mortality was common at the time.

In 1841, the family appear on the census in Clavering without Richard. Several hundred Essex men, perhaps Richard among them, were away from their home parish that June, sleeping in barns while they worked as haymakers.

Clavering cottages.

The first to die

When he was about eight years old, Joseph Chesham started to work for Thomas Newport at Curls Manor Farm in Clavering. Two years later, in December 1844, Thomas found two eggs in Joseph's pocket, which the boy claimed were given to him by his mother. On summoning Sarah, Newport asked her if this was true. Sarah denied it, and Thomas, deciding that Joseph had stolen from him, turned the boy away. Without work, Joseph, now aged ten, was sent to school.

Thomas Newport might have had things on his mind. A couple of months earlier at Michaelmas, the usual time of year for hiring servants and farm workers, his mother had employed a new housemaid. Lydia Taylor came from the nearby village of Manuden, the daughter of an agricultural labourer. She was seventeen, and Thomas, a bachelor nearly ten years her senior, sexually propositioned her just two weeks after she started work. Lydia initially put off his advances. It was certainly not unknown for masters and servants to become sexually involved; with a mixed group of people living under one roof, it was perhaps inevitable. The question is, how much mutual affection was involved in these situations – how much did the masters take advantage of servants, who caved in to their pestering for fear of losing their job?

In January 1845, Joseph Chesham was on his way home from school one afternoon when he got up on a bank to pick up a stick. Thomas Newport appeared – the Chesham's cottage was on his land so he was perhaps never far away. It was claimed that he grasped the stick and hit Joseph with it twice. Joseph went home and told his mother, who apparently said, 'You and I are always in somebody's way, and it would be a good job if we were both in the churchyard.' This would turn out to be a painfully prescient remark.

Joseph was in low spirits: he didn't want to eat and 'said he should never want any supper again, and went to bed crying.' That evening, he fell ill. The Chesham's neighbour, Thomas Deards, asked what was wrong. Sarah told him about Thomas Newport hitting her son, and that Joseph was 'so afraid of Mr Newport, that when he struck at him the boy ran forward to get out of his way, and I fear he has hurt something in his inside.'

His brother James also became ill; Philip, the Chesham's eldest son, complained of a headache, and John was sent home by his master with stomach pains. Joseph and James suffered most, vomiting in such quantity that it poured down through the bedroom floorboards into the 'lower room' of Thomas Deards's cottage, and his wife was in tears as she scrubbed it up on her hands and knees with old cloths. It was so intense that the neighbours could hear the children groaning in their sickness through the thin walls.

Deards challenged Sarah when he met her in the lane, saying, 'Are you aware how bad your children are? We can scarcely live in the house.'

According to Deards, Sarah exhibited detachment from the woes of her sick children, and prevaricated in sending for the doctor.

Richard Chesham, the boys' father, went to see Stephen Clayton Hawkes, a surgeon who lived at Clavering. He told Hawkes that the boys were very ill and Hawkes sent Richard away with a medicine that contained calomel. Calomel – mercurous chloride – is no longer used in medicine, but until the early twentieth century had a variety of uses, including as a purgative. Forcing the body to void itself of whatever ailed it was a standard Victorian method.

But it was too late for Joseph: he died on the evening of Sunday, 19 January, after a couple of days' illness. Monday morning at half-past six, the village in mid-winter darkness, Richard Chesham arrived at Hawkes's house to report his son's death; Hawkes decided to pay the Cheshams a visit.

Hawkes went upstairs and found Joseph's body laid out on the bed; downstairs he found James. He spent fifteen minutes with the ailing child, who complained of pain in his bowels and vomiting, and Hawkes gave him an aperient – a gentle laxative. The surgeon visited again at midday, and seeing no improvement in James's condition, he gave him a combination of opium and calomel. Hawkes made a third visit at about 7.00 pm, and saw that James was getting worse. As he had not seen Joseph in his illness, Hawkes suggested to Sarah that he perform an autopsy on her dead son, just to be sure of what had killed him – no cause of death was entered on the death certificate. 'She made no reply, although she appeared very reluctant,' Hawkes later said.

On Tuesday, Hawkes was informed that James had died too. The surgeon believed it was English cholera that had killed James, and this went on the death certificate, even though English cholera was unusual in the winter months and rarely fatal.

Mary Pudding, who made Sarah's mourning clothes after her sons' death, suggested that the coroner would be able to explain what had killed her children so suddenly, but Sarah replied that if the coroner came, 'my children would be opened, and I could not bear to see them cut about.'

To save expense the two brothers were placed in the same coffin and were laid to rest in the churchyard on 25 January 1845. Sarah was desperate with grief; a neighbour later commented that after her sons' deaths 'she was always very wild and comical; she looked so wild about her eyes that they appeared as if they would turn out of her head.'

Lydia Taylor's baby

Just after Whitsun in 1845, Thomas Newport's mother noticed that Lydia Taylor was in the family way. Lydia told her that Thomas was the father, and it was only at this point that Thomas realised Lydia was to have his child. He told her that he would fetch some medicine from the market town of

Bishop's Stortford, some 7 miles from Clavering. This, he promised her, 'would take it all away in a few days.' He returned and had something in his pocket – he did not show her what, and Lydia refused to take it. Moral and legal scruples might have prevented her from using an abortifacient, but as they were usually poisonous, she may have feared the physical damage it could cause.

The pregnant Lydia was dismissed from her post on the Newport's farm and returned to Manuden. Her mother, now with an extra mouth to feed and another on the way, approached the Newports for money and on various occasions Thomas gave her half-crowns and half-sovereigns. Solomon, Lydia's illegitimate son, was born in December 1845; the birth left Lydia very ill but three weeks later, having not left her bed, she received a visitor.

What follows is from evidence Lydia gave at the inquest and the trial. She claimed to be surprised to see Sarah Chesham – 'I had not spoken to her above twice before in my life.' With baby Solomon on her knee, Sarah poured scorn on Thomas Newport. He was, she said, 'a surly good-for-nothing fellow, and ought not to have done so.' The man who had beaten her son had fallen further in Sarah's estimation, taking advantage of a young woman in his service. Sarah spent nearly an hour in the Taylor's cottage and promised she would return, even though Lydia said she was too ill to cope with visitors.

Five weeks later, while Lydia was still bed-bound, Sarah visited again. She brought a rice pudding, an apple turnover, tea and sugar. Apparently eager to help, Sarah said she would make something for the child to eat, and despite Lydia's protestations that her mother had already fed him, Sarah took Solomon downstairs. Lydia hurried out of bed and found Sarah had been feeding the baby. She was wiping her fingers down her gown, and inside the fender, Lydia saw that Solomon had vomited.

They enjoyed quite a gathering that lunchtime, supping on Sarah's gifts – as well as Lydia and her mother, their party included a neighbour and Lydia's sister-in-law. Sarah made some food for the child, but after he had eaten it, she commented, 'Lor' dear he is come all over as callow as a rat.'

Lydia, seeing that her little boy was unwell, asked Sarah what she had fed him.

'Nothing but a piece of sugar,' she replied.

Lydia took her child from Sarah. He was sick, his lips white and slimy, and his mouth fell open 'as if he was dead.' Lydia put him in his cradle and wept over him – he appeared to be having convulsions.

Later, Lydia said that Sarah laughed; a sinister interpretation can be placed on this, unless it was the amusement of an experienced mother at a young mum's panic. After they had drunk some beer, which Sarah had sent for, the women's lunch came to its conclusion. Lydia claimed the apron she had lent Sarah on her visit had spots on it afterwards, and that on washing it the following day, it dropped to holes.

Solomon had been a healthy child, but Lydia alleged that after Sarah's first visit in January 1846, he sometimes appeared to be in violent pain. Despite her later claims that Sarah had injured her son, in May 1846 Lydia went to visit Sarah, taking her baby and her younger sister. As if intentionally baiting Thomas Newport, Sarah took the child upstairs and stood by the window with him, waiting for Thomas to pass. Then she changed her mind and decided to go across the fields to confront him with his misbegotten child.

Lydia, having paused to put on her bonnet, was a few steps behind Sarah as she ran up the field, Solomon's head bouncing over her shoulder. Unsurprisingly, a trail of the baby's vomit was in her wake. When Lydia caught up with Sarah and the baby, Sarah said she couldn't see where Thomas Newport was. Lydia decided she did not want a confrontation with her child's father. On taking Solomon back, she noticed something pink around his mouth. Lydia asked what it was and Sarah replied that it was, 'nothing but a piece of sucker'.

When Lydia put the child to bed in Sarah's cottage, he appeared unwell again. After a while, Lydia set off for home and Sarah walked with her, carrying Solomon for part of the journey. She thought Sarah was trying to put something in Solomon's mouth again, and the child was sick – Sarah denied giving him anything. Lydia told Sarah not to come to her family's house again, and all through the night Solomon was ill and apparently in great pain.

In June 1846, a few weeks after her visit to Sarah Chesham's cottage, Lydia went into service at Mr Welsh's in Stansted. The very next day, Sarah Chesham visited the Taylor's cottage. Lydia's mother told Sarah that she felt ill after attending two deaths, and Sarah, holding with the miasma theory of 'bad air' causing infection, put it down to her being poisoned by putrefaction from the bodies.

Mrs Taylor needed to check on her turkeys, so Sarah volunteered to help with the baby. Sarah disappeared out of sight, and Lydia's mother 'found she had "whipped" round a corner; I could see her standing with one foot on the bank, with the baby in her lap, and she appeared to be putting something into its mouth.' Sarah denied giving the child anything, and Solomon's grandmother said that his chin had dropped, his eyes were closed, and he appeared to be dying. There was white dribble around his mouth.

The child vomited when she got home so the doctor, George Welsh, was sent for. The grandmother told him that Solomon had been poisoned, but all the surgeon saw was a baby sleeping soundly in its cradle. Lydia's mother told Welsh that she believed Sarah had given Solomon something, but he later said that when he woke the child, 'it did so in a natural way, and I saw nothing the matter with it; I said I did not consider the prisoner had given the child anything.' Even so, Solomon's health deteriorated.

On 8 August, Thomas Newport was summoned before the bench of magistrates at Saffron Walden petty session and an order was made that he should pay two shillings and sixpence a week for his son's maintenance. Lydia's mother produced a letter from Mr Bowker, a solicitor from Bishop's Stortford, 'which subsequently led to suspicions of a case of poisoning; that case was then sufficiently gone into for a warrant to be granted.'

'Wholesale poisoning in Norfolk'

What had suggested poisoning to Lydia Taylor and her mother? During the early summer of 1846, there were reports of several deaths by arsenic poisoning in the Norfolk village of Happisburgh, about 100 miles north-east of the Taylor's home. Jonathan Balls was a rather odd, elderly man, and when he died suddenly, the coroner ordered an inquest. Jonathan was found in his coffin with his hands full of plum cake; he had also been buried with two walking sticks, a fire poker and the toys of his recently deceased granddaughter. A post-mortem showed that he had died of arsenic poisoning, and other sudden deaths in his family were investigated. Nine more bodies were exhumed, and in five, beside Jonathan's, arsenic was found. Evidence at the inquest pointed to Jonathan as the murderer.

The press filled their pages with exaggerations, claiming twenty people had been exhumed, all of whom were killed with arsenic. Their exaggerations, particularly in *The Times*, seem designed to highlight the problems of penny-pinching counties such as Norfolk, where 'the parish officers throughout the county had received a circular from the magistrates requesting them to make strict enquiries before the expense of an inquest was incurred, there having been a deal of complaint at the magistrates' meetings as to the heavy expense of coroners' inquests.'

Solomon Taylor fell ill at a time of fear and paranoia over arsenic. His mother's reaction has echoes of seventeenth-century witchcraft allegations, too. Rather than consider her child's illness to have an ordinary source, she took the line of reasoning favoured by Essex villagers 200 years earlier. If a villager was heard to utter a curse as they passed their neighbour's cows, and if one of those cows then became ill, the owner would reason that the curse had caused the sickness. Witchcraft allegations often involved the illness or death of children. Because Solomon's illness began around the time Sarah Chesham had visited, Lydia blamed her, and with secret arsenic poisoning on people's minds, Lydia alighted on the means that Sarah had apparently used.

Arrest

Sarah Chesham was arrested on 11 August 1846 and taken to Newport police station, about 4 miles east of Clavering. Essex was one of the first counties to adopt the new police system – the Essex Constabulary was established in 1840, a year after the Rural Constabulary Act was passed. For hundreds of years before, England was policed by part-time, non-professional constables who were farmers or shopkeepers, taking on the role for a year at a time. They had to administer the Poor Law, survey highways and work as churchwardens. Towns had nightwatchmen, and to track down smugglers, who were rife along the Essex coast, there was the Coastguard, known as the Prevention Service – unlike today, their role did not include saving lives at sea.

It was the idea of Home Secretary Robert Peel – after whom 'bobbies' get their nickname – to set up what became the Metropolitan Police in the 1820s, based partly on the gendarmes of France and the city police in Glasgow and Dublin. London was growing quickly and there was a perceived increase in crime; unrest followed the Napoleonic Wars, with food riots caused partly by

PC William Barnard of the Essex Constabulary, 1870s. The uniform was little changed from the 1840s.

the Corn Laws, as well as disorder caused by striking workers and political agitators such as the Chartists. Emphasis was placed on the prevention of crime, so beat patrols replaced the nightwatchmen. The Peelers' uniform was designed to make them look as little as possible like soldiers, so they were decked out in reinforced top hats and swallow-tail coats, with minimum decoration. The only weaponry they were allowed was a truncheon or, in an emergency or on a dangerous beat, a cutlass; inspectors were allowed to carry pistols. The Metropolitan Police worked in London but were sent into the provinces to quell rioting.

Eventually, unrest outside London led to the establishment of county constabularies along the lines of the Metropolitan Police. The East Anglian agricultural workers' fondness for arson may have contributed to Essex setting up its force so quickly. Despite Peel's attempts to avoid the police appearing too militaristic, many officers were recruited from the armed forces, as well as from the Coastguard – Captain McHardy, who came from the Royal Navy, was Essex's chief constable. He figured prominently in an 1853 Select Committee into county constabularies, after protests from ratepayers that the new police were too expensive and went out of their way to seek offences to investigate. Essex was held up as an example of how a county constabulary should be run. It was the opinion of the superintending constable of Oxfordshire, which was still using the old system, that 'six constables from the Essex force would be the equivalent of the seventy parish constables now under his supervision.'

The keenly efficient bobbies of the Essex Constabulary were on the case, faced with a bewildering quantity of local gossip and rumour. A surgeon examined medicaments taken from Sarah Chesham's house, and an investigation took place at the police station. Sarah was accused of attempting to poison Solomon Taylor, but what motive could Sarah have for murdering another woman's child? 'It had been generally rumoured and whispered about that this woman had been the agent of some party for getting rid of the child' – that agent was suspected to be Thomas Newport.

Lydia brought out the story of Thomas Newport encouraging her to procure an abortion – this was her proof that Thomas had encouraged Sarah to poison her child, as if a man who wanted a woman to abort her child would want it murdered once it was born. And who better to employ for so dark a deed than another woman?

Sarah's arrest caused much local excitement 'owing to the suspicions of its being mixed up with other matters of a very dark appearance' – the deaths of her own sons over a year earlier. Two medical men, George Welch and Samuel Welch, gave differing evidence; George had thought nothing amiss, whereas Samuel Welch felt that Solomon's health had deteriorated, having been born a strong child. Lord Braybrooke, one of the magistrates, said that it was one of the most difficult cases he had ever faced, and decided that Sarah would have to be sent to the next assize to stand before a judge and jury.

Sarah cuts a lonely figure: no one came forward to stand bail for her, and 'neither during the examination, nor since she has been in custody, has her husband been to see her, or sent anyone to enquire about her.' The tone implies that her guilt was a foregone conclusion – her community and her own family had disowned her.

The results of the medicaments analysis ends the report from the *Chelmsford Chronicle* in damning, cliffhanger style: they had been found to contain prussic acid, laudanum and arsenic. Surely this was proof of her guilt?

With so much suspicion in the air, and with authorities still smarting after the criticisms following Happisburgh, Joseph and James Chesham were exhumed on 17 August. It caused a great sensation in the neighbourhood, and according to possibly exaggerated press reports, from 700 to 1,000 people congregated around the churchyard and the Fox and Hounds inn, where the inquest was to take place. It was quite usual at the time for inquests to be held in pubs – they were local meeting spaces, the 'public house', after all. Writing his memoirs, nineteenth-century barrister William Ballantine (whom we shall meet later) had a low opinion of inquests, remarking that they must be an embarrassment to the police, 'conducted by incompetent officers, at some low pothouse, where all the gossip of the neighbourhood finds vent.'

Far from being a 'low pothouse', the Fox and Hounds, a friendly village pub, is still open today. Partially weatherboarded outside, inside it has low ceilings and exposed beams with metal tankards dangling from hooks. It feels as if it hasn't changed much since 1846, when C.C. Lewis, the coroner, assembled his jury of locals, and the police lined up their witnesses.

The Fox and Hounds, Clavering.

The condition of the boys' remains varies in the newspapers reports. The *Chelmsford Chronicle* said they 'were not so decomposed as might have been expected,' whereas the *Essex Standard* said, 'of course [they] were in an advanced state of decay.' Arsenic was thought to preserve corpses, so the outward appearance of the exhumed bodies was gruesome yet important to report, as it could immediately indicate to the reader whether or not the children had been poisoned. But there was only one way to be sure: their viscera were removed, carefully packaged and sent to London for the expert eye of Professor Taylor.

Victorian newspapers

On 20 August, the story of the Manuden and Clavering poisonings hit the newspapers, appearing first in *The Times*. As a daily paper subject to the one penny Stamp Tax, its price was inflated beyond most people's means and was aimed at the middle and upper classes. It adopted a snooty tone about the 'lower orders' who were not its main customers, but as it was printed on superior paper it could survive passing through the hands and under the eyes of many, so could be read by all classes of society.

In Essex there were weekly papers, which were more affordable for ordinary people – the *Chelmsford Chronicle* and the *Essex Standard*. These newspapers are still with us today, as the *Essex Chronicle* and the *Essex County Standard*. Snippets of news from around the country appeared in weeklies, but their focus was on local events. They cut and pasted news from other papers, which meant if errors and exaggerations appeared in the source, generally London papers like *The Times*, they would be repeated hundreds of times and pass into fact.

There was a culture of listening to the news as well as reading it first-hand: there were many who, if they could not write, could at least read, so most completely illiterate people would know someone who could read to them. Reading aloud to an audience from newspapers, as well as from books, was a feature of eighteenth- and nineteenth-century life. If you could not afford to buy your own newspaper and were hungry for news, you could head to your local coffee house or pub. The radical William Cobbett believed that newspapers were a bigger draw for publicans than their beer, and some pubs employed people to read the newspapers aloud for the benefit of other customers. There must have been an exciting frisson for anyone reading a report in the *Chelmsford Chronicle* about an inquest in the Fox and Hounds while drinking a pint in the very pub the inquest had taken place in.

'All the gossip of the neighbourhood'

The Times's first article on the events in Clavering and Manuden contains various inaccuracies – they called the prisoner Sarah Chesman, as did the *London Daily News*. They gave Lydia Taylor's name as 'Sarah Taylor', and said the 'Chesmans' lived in Littlebury, rather than Clavering. The very next day, they reported on 'The Poisoning at Clavering' again, this time calling the prisoner Sarah Cheesman. They said Sarah was 'on a charge of attempting to poison a child belonging to another woman, by rubbing a quantity of salve over and in its mouth, which was found to be impregnated with arsenic.' Although there were salves in Sarah's possession that did contain poison, as there were in medicine chests up and down the country, no one had proved she had rubbed those particular medicaments on Solomon's mouth: *The Times* had jumped to conclusions.

The same article said that after exhuming Sarah's sons, a third, unidentified, body was exhumed and the stomach sent to Professor Taylor for analysis as well. This isn't true at all, but the *London Standard* and other papers as far away as Chester repeated this story, copying it from the *London Gazette*, which seems to have copied it from *The Times*. And as in *The Times*, they all stated as fact that Sarah had rubbed an arsenic salve over Solomon's mouth.

The papers that carried the error about the third body do not appear to have printed a correction; that was up to the *Chelmsford Chronicle*: it 'is without foundation in fact, but other cases of poisoning, it is expected, will yet be developed, and the police are actively engaged in making further enquiries.'

What is true is that Professor Taylor had analysed the viscera of Sarah's two dead children, and had found them to contain arsenic. The stomach of Joseph, the first to die, contained from eight to ten grains of arsenic (520–650mg), more than enough to kill an adult, and James's contained even more – from twenty to thirty grains (1,300–2,000mg), which was enough to kill three or four adults. Considering that this is what was left after their violent vomiting and purging, the original amount the boys had consumed would have been quite large.

The inquest reconvened at the Fox and Hounds at ten o'clock in the morning, and 'long before the hour of meeting arrived, a number of respectable people congregated in parts of this generally secluded and rural village.' Sarah's husband Richard waited in the pub's yard and was spotted by a local reporter. 'There was nothing particular in his demeanour or appearance to lead an ordinary observer to imagine that he was connected at all with the proceedings of the day, beyond the many others of the labouring class standing about anxious to hear the result of the examination of the stomachs of the deceased.' What did his indifference signify? Did he think his sons had died of natural causes, so had no reason to suspect his wife of so horrible a crime?

'It is believed,' said the *Chelmsford Chronicle*, 'that the prisoner herself is altogether unaware of the exhumation of her two children and the subsequent enquiries; and while the general opinion is that her husband is entirely innocent of the atrocious crime alleged to have been committed by his wife, and in his own house, the utmost indignation prevails against the inhuman wretch, who there is every reason to suspect thus so secretly destroyed her own unoffending offspring. The medicaments and salves found in her possession [have been] found to contain arsenic also.'

So much for innocent until proven guilty: local rumour and now the evidence of what had caused her sons' death was, to media and locals alike, irrefutable proof of murder.

Scientific fact nudged up against village gossip, the new world colliding with the old. Professor Taylor, man of science, had come up from London, presumably by train. Passenger trains were not new in the 1840s, but the boom in that decade, with stations and lines linking up the country mile by mile, excited the Victorians. Newport Station, the nearest to Clavering and perhaps where Professor Taylor arrived, had only opened the year before, to great celebration – a band played, bunting fluttered and the locals cheered as the first train pulled in. Professor Taylor would not have been met with such a reception, but turning up in small, provincial stations to head to an inquest was part of his job.

But before one of Britain's leading chemists was able to speak, the meeting was treated to village bickering. The grandmother of Joseph and James – Sarah Chesham senior – was asked by the coroner, 'Has any woman told you that she knew all about it?' Yes – one; Lydia Newman had said to her, 'It was a sad thing for Sarah' and she 'knew all about the matter. She said it was a bad job she did not know better.'

'Lor', neighbour Chesham,' Lydia Newman protested, 'I never said no such thing.'

After being pressed by the coroner, Lydia Newman said that once she had met Sarah Chesham in the town, and 'she said she felt so bad she did not know what to do.' Were these the words of a panicked woman whose crimes were about to be discovered, or a bereaved mother struggling to cope with her grief?

Professor Taylor described his finds, the newspaper reporting it in technical language. He had found yellow arsenic in their stomachs – arsenic trioxide, which had turned into arsenic trisulphide after reacting with sulphur as the bodies decomposed. It was, he was sure, administered during life. To demonstrate, there in the local pub he produced parts of the boys' stomachs on glass slides and pieces of copper gauze from his analysis. After giving evidence, Taylor cautiously packed away the forensic material and the coroner requested it be kept safely in Taylor's care. Then 'the learned professor returned to London directly.'

Hawkes and Thomas Deards gave their evidence about the progression of the boys' illness. At the end of the meeting, the coroner considered Thomas's to be of the utmost importance as it seemed to show that Sarah had callously avoided sending for medical help for her children. The facts about the children's vomit coming through the floorboards was used to emphasise how ill they had been, although it clearly says much about the poor condition of their cottages.

It was important at the inquest to establish exactly when the children had fallen ill, but the evidence of Thomas Deards's wife, Elizabeth, who said that Joseph was too ill on the Friday before his death to eat his supper, contradicted that of Lydia Newman, who insisted that Joseph had arrived at her cottage in perfect health on Saturday evening to buy bread.

John Chesham, the second eldest Chesham boy, aged fourteen, was asked about the events of that weekend. He remembered Joseph and James coming down to dinner on the Sunday, but that neither could eat, and they were thirsty, which is a classic symptom of arsenic poisoning. He said there was no arsenic in the house, even though they did have rats. He was asked if his brothers had been out of work for a while, and he said they had – this question implied there was a financial motive for murdering two boys who were no longer paying their way. He was asked if someone had spoken to him about coming to the inquest, and John said someone had, but claimed he didn't know who they were. The coroner didn't believe him, so the boy was held in custody by the police present in the pub until being interviewed again. Threatened with transportation for perjury, John still refused to give a name, remaining 'doggedly and sullenly silent', but he did admit the mystery person had talked to him about arsenic. John's master, Mr Glasscock, said that at the same time as Joseph and James were ill, he had sent John home with stomach pains. 'This the boy persisted in denying to the utter disgust of the whole court.'

Mary Pudding had seen Sarah three weeks after the boys' death, and she talked about Sarah's reluctance for a post-mortem; 'She cried bitterly when it was mentioned that the coroner was coming.' Mary reported that Sarah had told her, when Joseph came home after being hit by Thomas Newport, that they were in the way and were better off dead – this was treated as suspicious, rather than as a figure of speech. She also told the inquest that Sarah had said she 'should never be happy in this world again, when she thought her children had been snatched away from her by the neglect of Mr Hawkes.' Hawkes protested, and the coroner replied that Hawkes should have visited the children as soon as their father came for help.

In order to divine the source of the arsenic, Margaret Minott, postmistress, and William Law, local rat-catcher, gave evidence. Sarah Chesham had approached both of them for arsenic, but they had not given her any. Margaret had forgotten to get it on her daily trip to Newport, and William 'did not fancy to let her have any.' Did he think that Sarah was a would-be poisoner? No – William said he didn't think Sarah would pay him adequately.

Nineteenth-century arsenic bottles.

Thomas Newport confirmed that he had dismissed Joseph, but didn't admit to beating him, although he did say that Sarah had approached him to talk about it. He was asked if he had arsenic – he did, but he kept it locked up.

The coroner adjourned the inquest. It was obvious the boys had been poisoned, but there was no proof where the arsenic that killed them had come from. 'They must not leave a stone unturned to get more evidence on that point. He would have every house enquired at, every shop visited, and the whole country scoured from beginning to end but they would find it out, if possible.'

The curious incident of the dog and the mysterious stranger

When the inquest was resumed a fortnight later, the evidence spiralled further into the murky regions of hearsay and gossip. Sarah's son Philip was called to give evidence. He was asked about his brothers' last days, and whether there was poison in the house. He said there wasn't. He was asked about food prepared by his mother, but none she prepared for him had an ill effect on him. A rumour had got about Clavering that Philip had had a puppy that died suddenly after eating food prepared by Sarah: a practice run, poisoning the family pet before poisoning her children, but Philip claimed the last food the dog ate had been prepared by their father.

Elizabeth Deards claimed that on the Sunday when Joseph and James were ill, Sarah had said, 'I shall soon hang on Chelmsford gallows and be buried underneath it.' Elizabeth's evidence gives a measure of Sarah's grief; that Sarah took on a rather wild appearance, and 'after their deaths she was always crying, and I said, "You always think about those poor boys"; and she said she always would.'

Reverend George Brookes, Clavering's parish priest, reported that Sarah told him Joseph and James had died of violent inflammation of the lungs, and she had complained about the way Thomas Newport had treated them.

Charles Cole, an employee of Thomas Newport, was asked to give evidence. Initially claiming he had no idea why he had been called, he eventually admitted that he had spoken to John Chesham before the previous meeting, and that a woman called Susan Green had also been present. Charles, then, was the mysterious stranger, and Susan said that on the night before the last inquest, she had heard John talking to Charles.

Susan claimed she had heard John say, 'Oh, I know what to say, for my master has told me.'

The coroner decided that John had been 'tampered with' by his employer, Wisbey, who happened to be a member of the inquest's jury. When challenged, Wisbey claimed that all he had said to the boy was that he should tell the truth. Another jury member, Stevens, said, 'It seems to me that you allow your servants to take a liberty with you which no servant of mine would dare to take with me. When that boy John Chesham left this room on the last enquiry, he touched you on the arm, looked up in your face and smiled. You then said, "Well done, boy, you did it very well."'

The coroner pointed out that everyone else at the previous meeting had thought that John, far from doing very well, had committed perjury. He asked Wisbey if the Newports had spoken to him about it, presumably meaning Thomas and his brother. Although Wisbey admitted to having visited them on their farm and that they had talked about the case, he denied they had mentioned John Chesham.

A juror asked, 'Did Thomas Newport say anything about arsenic?'

Wisbey replied, 'Yes, he said something about it, but I forget what.'

It would be odd if arsenic hadn't come up in conversations within a 10-mile radius of Clavering at the time. Stevens said that Wisbey's conduct had been disgraceful, 'and that his criminality had been increased by the fact that as a juror he had sworn to justice.' It was extremely difficult to find any impartial jurors where relationship networks wove the population together.

At the previous meeting, Sarah Chesham senior had claimed to have heard Lydia Newman cast aspersions; now it was Sarah senior's turn to be accused.

The coroner asked her if, since the last meeting, she had said, 'I was not going to tell them all I know.'

She denied this, but Spencer, a juryman, said, 'Mr Thomas Newport told me you said so in the presence of fifty people.'

Richard Chesham, the prisoner's husband, said that he was out at the nearby village of Littlebury on the Saturday before his sons died, and that the boys were ill when he got home. If it was believed that the boys fell ill on the Saturday, and not the Friday, then it could be suggested that Sarah had used her husband's absence to poison her children. On returning home, Richard went to Hawkes and told him that 'the children were very bad indeed.' Hawkes, perhaps to protect his himself, claimed Richard had said he didn't need to attend the children, but Richard denied this, saying he had asked Hawkes to come but the surgeon refused.

The coroner made his observations: they knew the dates on which the boys died and that they had been poisoned with arsenic, but was there any evidence to say how this had happened? The jury retired and deliberated for an hour and a half, then the coroner was called in and a further adjournment of five weeks was deemed necessary, 'from certain circumstances which have been disclosed, and of which until just now I was perfectly ignorant.'

But what were these circumstances? Clearly it was something that was known to at least one member of the jury, but the newspapers did not say.

Poisoner-for-hire

The Times decided to maintain their readers' interest, devoting several column inches on 21 September to exaggerations, assumptions and untruths. In their leading article that day, they recalled to their readers' minds the Happisburgh cases: the murderer in Norfolk had gone to his grave without facing justice, but at least in Clavering they had an accused poisoner who would get their day in court.

Although 'the suspected party in this case has still to await the verdict of a jury, we cannot assume the truth of all the particulars alleged against her,' they nevertheless made some astonishing claims as to Sarah's guilt. The accusations of Lydia Taylor had caused people to speculate on the sudden deaths of Sarah's children, but *The Times* declared that 'The village of Clavering seems to have long ago taken it for granted that the prisoner had poisoned her children, and yet they say little more about it than if she had killed her pigs. When she is once in custody, of course every tongue is loose' and that 'It is without question that an accepted and reputed murderess walked abroad in a village unchallenged and unaccused, and that all the inhabitants had seen her children buried without remark or outcry, though they were clearly convinced that there had been foul play.' But did the people of Clavering really think that Sarah had poisoned her children? It seems, from the evidence of the inquests, that this thought only crossed people's minds once Lydia Taylor's accusations were abroad.

The Times called Clavering 'an ignorant and secluded village' and said that Essex was 'an uneducated county' – even today, the British media don't flinch from negative stereotypes of the county. Without foundation, they claimed Sarah was a poisoner-for-hire 'whose employment was as well known as that of a nurse or washerwoman – who could put any expensive or disagreeable object out of the way, and who, as it was understood, had practised her infamous trade upon her own children.' They compared her to infamous Renaissance poisoners the Medicis and the Gonzagas and claimed the police had found in her house 'an assortment of poisons – ointments, powders, and the like – such as was discovered by Claudius in the private cabinet of Caligula' – a grand claim for medicaments that were perfectly legal and quite common to have in the house.

That Hawkes had stated Joseph's cause of death as 'unknown' and James's as 'cholera' allowed, *The Times* implied, someone to get away with murder due to the 'futile and defective' regulations for registering deaths. Certainly, the rules surrounding the registration of deaths in England and Wales at that time were lax; all it required was for whoever was present at the death, not necessarily the medical attendant, to report the cause to the registrar. With medical science still in its infancy, even the most experienced of medical practitioners would encounter cases where they had no idea what had caused someone to die. It wasn't unusual for a surgeon to report 'unknown' or 'by Visitation of God' as the cause and if they did not feel suspicious about the death it would go uninvestigated.

Then there was the behaviour at the inquest. 'Not only the mother[-in-law] of the accused, but other persons, unimplicated, as far as can be seen, in the transactions, have refused their own evidence to the Court, or given it grudgingly, and clearly without any aim at truth.' This, *The Times* claimed, 'would argue a depravity beyond even the ignorant unconcern which passes over murder as a thing of no moment.' Clavering, as it appeared in *The Times*, was a lawless place, where murderers wandered unchallenged, and where legal procedure was actively disdained.

The third victim?

The investigation was about to take a new turn: Solomon, Lydia Taylor's baby, died on 27 September. Sarah was already awaiting trial at the next assize for attempting to poison him; another inquest was opened on 30 September.

Lewis, who was overseeing the inquest into the Chesham boys' deaths, was the coroner in this investigation too. He and his jury assembled at the Cock Inn in Manuden, and then they headed across a mile of early autumn Essex countryside to the Taylors' unprepossessing cottage, 'a lone and wretched place, a mere hovel'. This was at odds with what they encountered once behind the front door, where they found 'an appearance of cleanliness and order which was not expected from the exterior'. To the Victorian reader, this signalled that the Taylors were the moral and worthy sort of working-class person, who scrubbed their flagstones and tried to live respectably. Waiting for them in the tidy environs of the Taylors' humble cottage was the emaciated body of Lydia Taylor's unfortunate child, lying in a 'neat plain coffin'.

Back at the Cock Inn, testimony was given by Lydia, her mother and her sister, Eliza. Samuel Welch, the surgeon, said that he had attended the birth and the child had been healthy, but Solomon had developed whooping cough. He didn't think that could have caused the stomach problems that had killed him. Having performed the post-mortem the day before the inquest, and showing the stomach in a bottle to those present, he believed that 'the immediate cause of death was inflammation of the stomach and bowels generally, but how induced he could not say.' The viscera were to be sent to 'some eminent chemist' – Professor Taylor.

The inquest met again on 10 October 1846. Two witnesses provided evidence that was little better than gossip – one had seen Solomon's grandmother crying while the child foamed at the mouth. He had said to Sarah Chesham, 'You are a sorrowful woman to serve that child so.'

Sarah, allegedly, replied, 'All I have done has been to give the child a piece of bread, and I picked it a bough, which it put into its mouth.'

John Cowell said he had seen Sarah 'in company with Mr T. Newport in improper situations'. Quite what these were, he did not say, but it would suffice to bolster any rumours that Sarah and Thomas were either having an affair or plotting to kill Solomon – or both.

The results of a detailed analysis by Professor Taylor of the medicaments from Sarah's house were reported. Three contained poison, 'but not of a dangerous character unless administered in large quantities.' One contained mercurial globules and nitrate of mercury, 'not a very active poison'. There were blistering flies (also known as Spanish flies), which was 'a powerful and active poison', and another ointment made from nitrate of mercury called golden eye salve, which was used for the cure of bad eyes. One of the jurors pointed out that Lydia Taylor had alleged Sarah had smeared pink ointment over Solomon's mouth, but this 'did not agree with the professor's report, which described it as yellow.' The coroner observed they were 'of a poisonous nature, but still used in medicine for other purposes'. Despite what *The Times* had fulminated, if owning such items led inevitably to a career as a poisoner, then almost every household in Victorian England harboured budding Lucretia Borgias.

At the end of October, the last meeting of the inquest into Joseph and James Chesham's deaths was held at the Fox and Hounds inn. Public interest had waned, despite Solomon's death, and few people attended other than the witnesses summoned by the coroner.

The evidence consisted purely of village gossip. James Player, a labourer who worked for Thomas Newport, said that early in the summer, before the investigation into the Chesham boys' deaths, he had gone by Sarah's house and seen her by the door. She was 'making a noise at her little boy,' and Player claimed that Sarah had said, 'Hold your tongue, you little dog, you ought to be where the other ones are.'

Player admitted that he had never heard Sarah say anything else and in fact had never had a conversation with her. But joining in with the local hoopla, he headed over to Manuden to tell Lydia Taylor what he had overheard. She backed him up, but said James had told her Sarah's words were, 'Damn you, you ought to go to sleep for half an hour with the other two.'

Lydia contributed more hearsay about Philip Chesham's dog, on whom Sarah may or may not have practised the art of poisoning. Apparently, Sarah had told Lydia that the dog had eaten some food she had cooked, and that she had tried to frighten it away with her apron; she then concealed the food from the dog under an umbrella. The dog tried to reach the food again, so Sarah shook the umbrella at the dog, 'which went under a bench, and it laid there and died in less than ten minutes.'

Lydia presumably thought she was proving that Sarah had poisoned the dog, but why would someone trying to surreptitiously poison a baby admit as much to the child's mother? Lydia reported that Sarah had said 'she thought she had fluttered the heart of the dog, by frightening it with the umbrella, as Tommy Newport had fluttered the hearts of her two boys.'

The newspaper reported the reaction to this in one word: sensation – that most Victorian of words, which introduces to the mind's eye a collective gasp; the holding up of lace-edged handkerchiefs; a swiftly uncapped bottle of smelling salts.

Philip Chesham was brought in and refused 'to kiss the book' and 'stared doggedly' at the Bible. The coroner asked him if anyone had told him not to swear on oath, but Philip denied this. He brightened up when the coroner asked if he remembered the dog dying, and he said that the dog had died after his brothers, but the coroner pointed out this contradicted the evidence he gave before.

Richard Chesham said the dog 'lived some time after the children died.' A lad called Chipperfield, an employee of one of the jurors, 'made a statement about the dog, Philip Chesham, and John Chesham, but Mr Spencer said it was quite different to what he had told him a fortnight before.' Perhaps they had forgotten when the dog died because it had seemed insignificant at the time. The animal was not exhumed to test for poison, and it wasn't mentioned again. The question as to whether it had been poisoned or not was never answered.

The coroner referred to there being a connection between Sarah and Thomas Newport, and that two material witnesses had been 'kept from them by unfair means, or they would have had evidence to prove that such was the case.'

But what exactly is the connection he alleged? One witness had said they were spotted in 'improper situations', but did this mean there was something sexual between them? As the Cheshams' cottage was on Newport's land, Sarah and Thomas could have met by chance quite easily, and if Sarah was convinced that he had killed her sons, she may have sought him out to hassle him.

The coroner expressed 'a hope that the jury would free their minds from all conversation which they had had on the subject' and rely solely on the evidence, delivering 'their verdict as their consciences might dictate to them'. But how could anyone in Clavering have come to a disinterested and purely objective decision? The verdict delivered after ten minutes' deliberation was wilful murder against Sarah Chesham.

The end of the first act was nigh: a few days later, the last meeting of the inquest into Solomon Taylor's death took place in Manuden. Whilst interest had flagged at the end of the Chesham boys' inquest, the verdict of wilful murder 'appeared to have re-exited the public mind on the subject of the strange investigations, and the room was filled.'

Professor Taylor's 'elaborate report' of Sarah's medicine chest was read out. He concluded 'that the administration of none of the poisons found could have produced the death of this child [and] from the state of the body there was nothing to form an opinion that death had been caused by poison, either directly or indirectly.'

The post-mortem had shown that Solomon had died of a disease of the mesenteric glands; Mr Brook, a surgeon from Newport, said it was 'a disease of which so many children died, it would be out of his power to conclude that the child died from the effects of poison. [He] saw nothing in the case to bring him to the conclusion that disease was produced by the administration of poison.'

The coroner, summing up, said that the child 'became ill, in a mysterious manner, lingered, and ultimately died.' Was it from natural causes or something given to the child by Sarah Chesham? What about the evidence that Thomas Newport wanted to get rid of him – was Sarah 'an instrument in his hands or not?' The doctors disagreed – Welch thought Solomon's stomach was inflamed, but Professor Taylor thought there was no inflammation at all. The 'case was full of suspicion,' and the coroner and the police had been prevented from procuring evidence 'by attempts to keep out of the way witnesses who could have given testimony. One person who came down by the railway to Stortford had been met at the train by three individuals, and there, to use a vulgar expression, had been made "all right", and no doubt at this moment was kept out of the way, and paid pretty handsomely to remain so.'

It took twenty minutes for the jury to decide 'that the deceased, Solomon Taylor, died from disease of the mesenteric glands, but whether from natural causes, or that it arose from violence, there was not sufficient evidence to show.'

A month before the close of the inquest into his death, Solomon had been buried in Manuden's churchyard. A pencil note in the margin reads, 'The supposed murder of Solomon Taylor was tried at Chelmsford on …' but the date and the trial's outcome was never added.

Lucretia

In November 1846, while Sarah Chesham languished in Springfield Gaol, Edward Bulwer-Lytton's novel *Lucretia* was published. Taking her first name from Lucretia Borgia, the legendary Renaissance poisoner, he tied his main character to contemporary England by giving her the surname 'Clavering'. He deliberately hitched his literary wagon to Sarah Chesham's alleged crimes, which had only come to light that August: unless he wrote at speed, Bulwer-Lytton must have gone back through his manuscript to change a previous surname in order to give his novel exciting contemporary resonance. It could even be that *The Times*'s leader, comparing Sarah Chesham to legendary poisoners of yore, had inspired the name of Bulwer-Lytton's main character.

Bulwer-Lytton was widely criticised for his novel, which he had based on the crimes of 1830s forgerer and poisoner Thomas Griffiths Wainewright. It was probably Professor Taylor, in the *Medical Gazette*, who wrote that it was a dangerous book – they had already written about 'the increase in the crime of assassination by poison in this country', linking it with 'the singular and pernicious inclination which has, of late years, sprang up among the novelists and minor historians of France and England'. He believed that poisoners were learning to refine their crimes, 'the result of the clear, though indirect, lessons which the literature of the day too amply affords the criminal.'

The Times wrote a long, scathing review of *Lucretia*, shot through with heavy-handed irony. They criticised Bulwer-Lytton's literary failings as much as the morals of writing such a book: 'Indeed, save in the Newgate Calendar, we never heard of so many murders in so few volumes, and none in the "Calendar" itself half so terrible and monstrous.' And of the novel's anti-hero, 'He comes upon the stage wicked, he walks through the piece wicked, he dies wicked for no earthly object that you can discern, unless it be the very legitimate one of sustaining the long since well-earned reputation of the domestic *melodrame*.'

Bulwer-Lytton, responding to the poor reviews of his book, penned a lengthy defence. Whilst newspapers might protest about crime and murder appearing in novels, they were quite happy to publish inquests and trials in great detail. Bulwer-Lytton was not prepared to let this hypocrisy pass unremarked:

> There exists a Press which bares at once to the universal eye every example of guilt that comes before a legal tribunal. In these very newspapers which would forbid a romance writer to depict crime with all that he can suggest to demonstrate its causes, portray its hideousness, insist on its inevitable doom, are everywhere to be found the minutest details of guilt, – the meanest secrets of the prison-house are explored, turnkeys interrogated, and pages filled with descriptions of the personal appearance of the felon, his dress at the bar, his courage at the gallows. To find the true literature of Newgate and Tyburn, you have only to open the newspaper on your table.

Did this battle of wits raging in the press penetrate through the walls of Springfield Gaol? Did Professor Taylor, having visited Clavering and met some of Sarah Chesham's family, believe she read pot-boilers like *Lucretia*?

Sarah's letter

Even if Sarah was able to read – the criminal register said her 'degree of instruction' was imperfect, rather than that she had no instruction at all – she couldn't write. Three days before Christmas, she asked Frances Hall, the matron of Springfield Gaol, to write down a letter for Thomas Newport that she wished to dictate.

> 'Sir – Mr Bowker informed me, when I saw him last, that my friends would keep me with money to board myself; he left me a half-sovereign.

Mr Bowker said he would call again by the time that money was spent; but I have not seen him since. I know it is not in my own friends' power to keep me, therefore you must; for, Mr Newport, you well know that you promised me, when we stood against Pond-field gate together, that I should want for nothing. – that what I wanted I was not to stand for any expense, for you would pay it. You told me not to speak of it; but now I must, for you won't send to me, nor let my own relations come to see me; for 'tis you, and you only, that keep them from me. You know you ruined me, and have brought me to all this trouble, and you know 'tis true, and my friends know the same. I wish I had told you all about it when I was at Newport Station, for if I had spoke truth then you must have been in prison as well as myself. You deserve to be here more than I do, for you did it, not me; and you know that I have told you that I would speak of it times and times, and you told me not to be a d----d fool; for I told you I would have a letter wrote and keep it by me for fear anything should happen to me, for I always told you you would be the death of me, and so I say now. 'Tis your money keeps you out of prison – you deserve to be here more than me. Mr Newport, you shall support me, for I am suffering for the crime that you did. You caused the death of my poor children. I am wretched, and always shall be, for you know what I have upon my mind; and I cannot never be happy any more, and if you do not suffer in this world you will in the next. You know this is all true and much more if I could be allowed to send it. From the unhappy

Sarah Chesham.

P. S. – I hear I am going to be brought in fault about Sarah Parker, at Wigill's, but you know it was yourself did that.

Wells handed it to the governor of the gaol, who passed it on to Lord Braybrooke, the magistrate. From him, the letter made its way to the Home Office.

The letter can be read to suggest there was a conspiracy of some sort between Sarah Chesham and Thomas Newport, and those who believed that she had been paid by him to poison Solomon Taylor would have leapt on this letter as a near-confession. But notice that she does not mention the baby at all, and says, 'You caused the death of my poor children.' We return to the allegation she made of him having hit Joseph; did she also suppose that he had poisoned her children too?

Another arrest

In January 1847, Thomas Newport was arrested by the appropriately named Inspector Shackell. The press were kept out of the magistrates' room at Newport police station, as was Thomas's brother, and even his legal advisor. The *Chelmsford Chronicle* tried to get to the truth by other means and said the charge was of Thomas 'having feloniously aided and abetted Sarah Chesham in the administration of poison to her two children.'

The newspapers were not given access to Sarah's letter at this point, and the report is muddled and referred again to the poisoning of Solomon Taylor, even though that wasn't what they said Newport had been charged with.

Thomas was committed to stand trial and was refused bail. As with the earlier inquests, there were accusations made that he was using his money and influence to ease his way. 'It was stated that Lydia Taylor had been discharged from her situation, owing to her having appeared as a witness against Newport, and that Cowell, another important witness, had been treated in a similar manner by the brother of the prisoner.' Had Lydia lost her job because the Newports leant on her employers, or did her employers not wish to be connected with these well-publicised cases?

At the Bail Court, Thomas's legal advisor challenged the decision that he should not be allowed bail. Once again, the facts published in the local paper are muddled – either the reporter was confused, or the legal advisor was.

The only evidence that appeared to affect [Thomas Newport] was a statement made that he had been acquainted with the female prisoner some five years ago, and that while she was in a state of pregnancy, he said that she ought to get rid of it. The children, however, did not die for months after they were born.

This blunder, conflating Sarah with Lydia, may have led people to assume that Sarah Chesham had been having an affair with Thomas Newport. It may even have darkened the interpretation of events involving Sarah's husband that were, as yet, three years distant.

Thomas Newport was granted bail at the Petty Session in February. He had already posted £400 as a surety that he would attend the next assize, and his solicitor applied for another, consisting of £100 from four other people: Thomas had wealthy supporters. The charge had altered from inciting Sarah Chesham to murder her two sons, to 'having incited Sarah Chesham to poison Solomon Taylor'.

In the very same issue, the *Essex Standard* reprinted an article from the *Medical Gazette* on the 'Increase of Secret Poisoning', blaming it on certain works of fiction and non-fiction. Slow poisoning, especially, they felt was a risk, as poison could be given in small doses over a long period of time, making the crime less obvious. This was precisely what Bulwer-Lytton had protested: no would-be poisoner needed novels to learn their skills when the newspapers could instruct them anyway.

The first trial

On Thursday, 11 March 1847, Sarah Chesham was taken from her cell in Springfield Gaol, where she had been for six months, to the Shire Hall in Chelmsford to stand trial. The grand Georgian-fronted edifice stands at the top of Chelmsford High Street. A multi-purpose building, it still houses the largest ballroom in Essex, and in Sarah Chesham's day, it was the site of a corn exchange too.

Defence counsel for those indicted for murder was a recent phenomenon; it was only since the Prisoners' Counsel Act in 1836 that defence counsel became almost universal in murder trials. Someone had to pay for it – if the prisoner could not it would fall to charity, or one of the barristers present at the trial on the day might step in for free.

Prosecution and defence counsel meant the introduction of expert witnesses, men like Professor Taylor who could be drafted in to present damning evidence. But defence counsel were often brought in late, so had little time to investigate themselves, basing their defence on reports from

Chelmsford Shire Hall.

the inquests, which they sometimes had to get from the near-verbatim newspaper reports. The idea that these reports prejudiced a fair trial was not dealt with for some years. Neither did the defence have much interaction with the accused: in his long career, William Ballantine recalled only once having interviewed a prisoner he was defending before they stood in the dock. The accused were not allowed to speak in court, other than to pass notes or whisper to their counsel. The defence were forced to think on their feet, their main weapons being clever questioning of witnesses and melodramatic closing speeches.

Overseeing the Essex Lent Assize was Thomas Denman who, as Lord Chief Justice, was the second highest judge in England and Wales. He was a Whig with liberal principles; he had worked with others towards abolishing the slave trade, and his defence of the Luddites demonstrated his sympathy for the working class. He was, perhaps, the most sympathetic judge Sarah could have had.

Leading Sarah's defence was Charles Chadwick Jones, Serjeant-at-Law, who had been a barrister for nearly twenty years. He was vastly experienced, having had an extensive practice at the Old Bailey bar, until he abandoned it in 1844 on becoming a Serjeant-at-Law. The prosecution was led by Montague Chambers, QC, grandson of an admiral and the son of an architect, with Thomas Chambers and Charles Wordsworth. Wordsworth was a first cousin of the poet, and was from Essex himself, having been born in Harwich. These grand men would decide the fate of an impoverished agricultural labourer's near-illiterate wife.

Denman arrived in Chelmsford in the usual great pomp afforded to an assize judge, travelling to the Shire Hall in the new Sheriff of Essex's carriage. He attended a service in the cathedral which the Shire Hall backs onto, where he heard a sermon about crime and punishment.

Sarah's trial began at nine o'clock in the morning, 'long before which hour the Court was thronged with crowds of persons anxious to obtain admission. The most intense interest was manifested in the proceedings and their result.' She was to be tried three separate times, starting with the death of Joseph Chesham. Several indictments were read out, and some of the jurymen were objected to and replaced.

Chambers' opening speech reminded the court of the seriousness of the crime for which Sarah stood accused and that 'it would be his duty to state certain expressions and acts of the prisoner, which might lead to the inference that she had not that kind disposition towards [her son] which ought to exist in the heart of a mother.'

The first witness was Margaret Minott, whom Sarah had approached a fortnight before her sons' deaths to buy arsenic. When cross-examined by Jones, Margaret said, 'I was on friendly terms with the prisoner as far as speaking; for anything I know [she] appeared a kind mother to her children.' Did Sarah have a rodent problem in her cottage? Margaret said she didn't know, but Sarah had told her so. Importantly, Margaret said, 'She did not make the least secret of applying to me for poison.'

Lydia Newman's brief testimony was that Joseph Chesham had gone to her house to buy bread on the evening before he died. Newman had given evidence at the inquests before, as her testimony was used to support the timeline – when exactly did Joseph Chesham fall ill? The witnesses contradicted each other, unsurprising when they were recalling events that happened more than two years before.

William Law, the rat-catcher, said that one evening he passed the Chesham's cottage, and Sarah said she 'wished I would lay some poison round her house to kill the rats.' But he didn't. However, he was quite sure that the Cheshams did have a rat infestation.

This was further backed up by their neighbour, Thomas Deards, who said, 'I was very much troubled with rats and mice, and I know that the Cheshams were too; we had to put our victuals out of the way at night for fear the rats should get it.'

Thomas's evidence of Sarah being outside the cottage while her children were ill, and her delay in sending for medical aid, was useful to the prosecutor to paint Sarah as a bad mother. But on the Sunday morning, Sarah had been going to church, contradicting the bad character the prosecution were trying to present. To further emphasise the laxity with which medical help had been sought, the churchwarden spoke. He said the Cheshams did not apply for an application for a doctor, but on another occasion when there was illness in the family, they had.

Deards reported how Sarah banged on the wall that Sunday evening, shouting, 'For God's sake get up, for my child is dying.' He found Joseph dead, and Sarah held 'a handkerchief before her face, and she appeared to be crying a little.'

Thomas Deards's wife Elizabeth added that when Sarah was taken into custody, she had asked Elizabeth to look after her son – presumably George, her youngest, who was seven years old. She repeated what she had said at the inquest, that Sarah said she would be buried beneath the gallows, but on being cross-examined, Serjeant Jones undermined her evidence by making Elizabeth admit that she was a little deaf. Sarah's comment might actually have meant 'that those who die of hard work would be buried under the gallows'.

It was the turn of Hawkes. The judge took him to task for his assumption that the boys had died of English cholera.

'Do you think yourself justified in certifying that which you did not know, and that an uncommon complaint at that time of year?'

'The symptoms were so like that I could not give any other,' Hawkes replied.

Denman was unrelenting. 'But you had no right to give any unless you knew it of your own knowledge.'

Hawkes later felt he had to defend himself from this attack on his professionalism, which was widely reported in the press. Writing to *The Times*, he explained that he had not given a cause of death for Joseph as he had not witnessed the child alive. Instead it was registered as 'unknown'. He neglects to mention that he gave cholera as the cause of death for James, even though it turned out to be wrong.

Reverend Brookes said he knew Sarah Chesham well, and that she 'spoke in very bitter terms against Mr Newport and his mother; she alluded to the charge of stealing eggs, … she said it preyed very much upon [Joseph's] mind and aggravated his complaint; that almost the last words he spoke was a message to his master or mistress that he never stole the eggs.'

Cross-examined by Sarah's defence, he said that, having visited the family soon after the children died, he found nothing unusual in their deaths. 'I went to the house without any suspicion of the death being unfairly caused, and came away under the same impression.' Asked what he thought of her as a mother, he replied, 'She appeared to be all that a mother ought to be.'

Mary Pudding repeated her evidence and said that Sarah blamed Hawkes for her sons' deaths. In cross-examination, she said, 'I never saw anything to the contrary of her being a good mother,' and when quizzed about Sarah's state of mind when she made her comment about them being in someone's way, 'she seemed to be in very great grief, like a mother who had lost two children.'

Frances Hall, the matron of the gaol, gave evidence about Sarah's letter. Serjeant Jones forced her to admit that she did not caution Sarah before writing it for her.

Then came the forensic evidence. It had to be proved that Professor Taylor had examined the stomachs of Joseph and James, so firstly Henry Brookes, who performed the autopsy and took the stomachs to London, gave evidence. He passed them to Professor Graham, who then had to give testimony that he had received them from Brookes and then passed them on to Professor Taylor. This unbroken chain was essential to show that the stomachs had not been tampered with and that they belonged to the right bodies.

Professor Taylor told the court that by the appearance of Joseph Chesham's stomach, from the symptoms described and the fact that his tests had yielded several grains of arsenic, 'I should infer, beyond all question, that death was caused by poison.'

This was the case for the prosecution. Serjeant Jones now addressed the jury 'in a forcible and eloquent manner', emphatic that the jury should be aware that if they found Sarah guilty, it was a case 'of that peculiar description in which no mercy could be extended', and that they should therefore be absolutely sure of their verdict. He mentioned that he had no warning about the evidence of Sarah's letter to Thomas Newport, but he insisted that it 'ought not to weigh a single feather in the scale' against her.

He emphasised that Sarah was thought of as a good mother, and as such, could not have murdered her own son. No motive had been presented for her to have committed 'so dreadful a deed', and he underscored the evidence of Reverend Brookes who, as a clergyman, was to be trusted in his assessment of Sarah's upright character and good mothering. He asked that they reached their decision only on the evidence they had heard in court 'and not allow themselves to be biased by any newspaper reports or by the idle, and he feared, in some instances, wicked rumours which had been circulated, he feared through almost the whole county of Essex for many months past.'

The judge summed up, and it was now up to the jury to reach a verdict. They had five to choose from: guilty of murder, guilty of murder but with a recommendation to mercy, guilty of manslaughter, not guilty by reason of insanity, or not guilty. After just ten minutes' deliberating in their box, the jury found Sarah Chesham not guilty.

'We have no doubt of the child having been poisoned, but we do not see any proof of who administered it.'

The second trial

The first case had already occupied several hours, and Montague Chambers said 'as it was an important matter he had no alternative but to proceed with the next charge'; a fresh jury was called and Sarah was tried for the murder of James Chesham.

Sarah's son Philip was the only new witness to give evidence. He 'appeared to have a great impediment in his speech, as well as giving his testimony most unwillingly.' He answered 'I don't know' to most of the questions put to him, which concerned the timing of James falling ill and the movements of his parents over that weekend. His ill-fated pet dog wasn't mentioned. When cross-examined, Philip replied, with heartbreaking simplicity, 'My mother has been a good mother to we.'

When it was time for the forensic evidence, it emerged that Professor Graham, essential to complete the chain of evidence regarding the stomachs, was on his way back to London. What then followed would have confirmed to the Victorians that they really were living in the future – 'the electric telegraph was employed to intercept him at Shoreditch, and his return was expected by the 5.41 train.' The Victorians of the 1840s found themselves in a world where a scientist could find arsenic in the secret interiors of the body, where a man could travel quickly by train, and where he could be summoned through the agency of electrical pulses sent down a wire.

There was a delay, but Professor Graham returned and the forensic evidence was given; after Jones's speech, the judge summed up and at seven o'clock in the evening, ten hours after Sarah Chesham had first been brought from her cell, the jury started their deliberations. It took them twenty minutes to find her not guilty.

The third trial

But there was one more case for Sarah to be tried on, and she spent another night in her cell. On Friday morning, she was brought back to the Shire Hall on the charge of 'administering poison to Solomon Taylor, an infant, and thereby murdering him; other counts laid it to be done with intent to murder him'.

Sarah's defence team made many objections to the jury, so many 'that the panel returned by the Sheriff was exhausted and a number of the town tradesmen had to be called in.'

Once again, Lydia Taylor went over her evidence; she 'cried bitterly' at certain points. Given Sarah's acquittal for the murders of Joseph and James Chesham, securing a conviction must have seemed hopeless.

In cross-examination, Lydia's morals were put into question – was Thomas Newport really the father of Solomon? Had Lydia not dallied with a man called William Taylor, a cowman on the Newports' farm?

'I will swear before you all I never had intercourse with him or with any other man.'

Sensation fluttered through the crowded courtroom, the sex life of a young servant girl laid out for all to hear. While Sarah's defence had invoked the figure of the good, loving mother, Lydia's character was undermined, presenting her as an untrustworthy floozy.

Lydia was insistent. Sarah Chesham 'has been the death of my child and nobody else.' But the belief of Lydia and her mother in Sarah's guilt was not enough. Professor Taylor gave his evidence, saying, 'There was no appearance to indicate that the stomach had been destroyed by any corrosive substance,' and the rest of his testimony demonstrated 'the entire absence of any poison in the stomach'.

Montague Chambers accepted defeat and said, after that evidence he could carry the case no further. The judge agreed, and the jury acquitted Sarah Chesham.

Although Sarah could now go home to Clavering, it wasn't over yet. Thomas Newport was supposed to stand trial at the same assize for his involvement in Solomon Taylor's death. Even though Sarah had been acquitted, for reasons that are not explained in the newspapers his trial was traversed to the next assize. Sarah's homecoming would have been marred by this lack of resolution: she had been cleared, but suspicion still clung to her.

Another Essex poisoning?

Sarah Chesham was not the only woman to stand trial for poisoning at the assize that spring. Sarah Bright from Little Dunmow was indicted for the murder of her illegitimate son, using 'a certain destructive liquid consisting of soap liniment and tincture of opium'. In a parallel to the Manuden case, the child's father, David Gray, was indicted for counselling her to murder the baby.

Sarah Bright gave birth to her son, David Gray Bright, on 20 November 1846 in Dunmow Union Workhouse. She returned to her parents not long afterwards, and 'conducted herself with all the tenderness of a mother.' The baby was taken ill with convulsions on New Year's Day, and died less than a fortnight later.

The death had been referred to a coroner's jury, who returned a verdict of natural death, 'but afterwards some circumstances came to light, and the magistrates thought it necessary to send the case before a jury.' Even the prosecution doubted there was enough evidence to secure a conviction. A surgeon, Mr Bell, had performed a post-mortem on the child and found him healthy apart from congestion in the brain, which would have caused the reported convulsions. He sent the child's stomach to Professor Taylor, along with a vial that a policeman had found: the vial contained opium, thirty drops of which could have caused death.

Bell explained that if the child had taken thirty drops, the spirits of rosemary in the soap liniment would have left a perceptible odour in the stomach, and it hadn't. Lord Denman decided that it was impossible to say if the child had been killed by anyone, so Sarah Bright and David Gray were acquitted. They went back to Little Dunmow and were married a year later.

Meanwhile, in Suffolk

For anyone disappointed by the lack of convictions for poisoning at the Lent Assize in Essex, they would have been cheered by the trial of Catherine Foster at Bury St Edmunds, nearly 50 miles north of Chelmsford. Catherine lived in Acton, Suffolk, only a few miles from the Essex border, between the mediaeval wool towns of Long Melford and Lavenham. Acton was an agricultural village, where most of the residents worked the land as labourers, and many of the girls went into service. Some found employment in nearby horsehair factories, where cotton was woven with horsehair to generate a strong, hard-wearing cloth.

Catherine was only seventeen when, in October 1846, she married John Foster. They had been walking out for a time, John meeting Catherine outside the village school after she had finished her lessons; once she found employment as a servant outside Acton, John would walk miles to visit her. But then she was dismissed and returned to her mother's cottage. John suggested he could move in as a lodger and Catherine's mother encouraged their marriage, concerned in case Catherine fell pregnant. John was keen to move because his parents' cottage was overrun by his sister's own illegitimate offspring, or 'chance children' as they are called in the newspaper reports.

Just three days after their wedding, Catherine went to Pakenham, 20 miles away from Acton, to visit her aunt. She stayed there a fortnight, which seems very odd for a newly-wed. Odder still, a few days after her return, her husband died.

Catherine had made a dumpling for him to eat on his return home from work one day, and he hadn't finished it before complaining of heartburn, and then ran into the yard at the back of the house to vomit. He developed diarrhoea along with vomiting, and the next day Catherine dawdled her way to Mr Jones, a surgeon at Long Melford. Just like Hawkes in Clavering, Jones diagnosed English cholera without seeing his patient, and prescribed a medication of chalk and rhubarb. John's condition worsened and he died the following day.

Mordecai Simpson, a relative of the author, was Catherine Foster's next-door neighbour. The Simpsons had chickens, which roamed the gardens behind the cottages. The chickens died on the same day as John Foster, after eating his leftover dumpling, which had been thrown outside. Their crops were examined and found to contain arsenic. A coroner's inquest was opened into John Foster's death, and his stomach was sent, not to Professor Taylor, but to a doctor in Bury St Edmunds called Mr Image. Catherine was sent to the gaol in Bury, where she waited five months until the Lent Assize.

Did Catherine, pacing her cell in Bury St Edmunds, know about the recent acquittals at Chelmsford? She was not to have the luck of Sarah Chesham or Sarah Bright – she was found guilty of murder. Petitions circulated calling for mercy, and an editorial in the *Bury & Norwich Post* declared capital punishment to be 'a blot upon our civilisation'. But on 17 April 1847, Catherine Foster was hanged by infamous Victorian executioner William Calcraft. An estimated 10,000 people gathered to watch the grisly scene as a

Jane Kemble, née Dewes (1859–1934), the author's great-great-grandmother. Mordecai Simpson was Jane's great-uncle.

teenage girl was strangled in full view of the public above the gates of Bury Gaol.

Why did this case have so woeful an outcome compared to those tried at Chelmsford only a couple of weeks before? In Catherine's case, there was evidence of the poison having been administered, which there wasn't in the cases tried at the Essex Lent Assize. The testimony came from her 9-year-old brother, who claimed that when preparing the dumplings, Catherine had used her own flour, rather than her mother's, and that she had taken a dark powder from a screw of paper and sprinkled it into the dough. This done, she threw the paper into the fire, apparently to hide the evidence.

While she awaited her execution, she confessed to having bought the arsenic from a shop in Sudbury, three days before preparing the fatal dumplings. But why did her brother say it was a dark powder when arsenic trioxide is white? And had she explicitly bought the arsenic for murder? It has been suggested that she may have wanted to use it as an abortefacient; it could even have been intended for her husband as an aphrodisiac. But just before her execution Catherine confessed to killing her husband, in a letter she wrote in her cell: 'I must confess that I ame gilty veary gilty of this awful criame.'

Thomas Newport on trial

Before the Essex Summer Assize, the Essex Quarter Session, dealing with money matters, took place. The cost of Sarah Chesham's prosecution was queried – it had cost £337. Of this, the coroner's expense was £9, for which sum he had travelled 500 miles. Sir John Tyrell, a Tory MP, pointed out that the unusually high cost was down to the case having been 'an extraordinary one, and there was immense excitement about it.' Another magistrate pointed out that 'the greater part of the expenses happened before the trial: there was adjournment after adjournment of the enquiry before the trial took place.'

How much excitement still existed is hard to tell, but the frisson of illicit sexual behaviour continued to cling on to Lydia Taylor's story. In the middle of July, Thomas Newport stood in the dock at Chelmsford Shire Hall, charged with a misdemeanour, 'by endeavouring to incite Lydia Taylor to use certain drugs to procure abortion.' There is nothing to indicate there was the same level of interest in this trial as there had been a few months earlier, but we might imagine the airless room, with the judge and barristers red-faced in their wigs and gowns in the summer heat. Thomas Newport, 'whose name was so prominently mixed up in the evidence against the woman Chesham,' pleaded not guilty.

Once again, Wordsworth was prosecuting. He explained to the jury that their decision would 'depend upon whether they believed the evidence of Lydia Taylor, and the way in which she told her story; and in the second place whether her statement received sufficient confirmation from any other party' – her mother.

Lydia Taylor was now Lydia Parker – a month before the assize, she had got married. Just as she had done on several previous occasions at the inquests, she gave her story about falling pregnant by Thomas Newport, and how he had insinuated that she should 'get rid of it'. She 'was in tears during the examination, and manifested some reluctance in giving her evidence.'

Her mother told the court how Newport had said 'it was a bad job, and [she] must try to get rid of it.' The judge queried, 'Is this the only evidence you can call of direct solicitation?'

'Yes, my Lord,' Wordsworth replied. Lydia was not giving 'the most stringent part of her story'.

The judge decided there wasn't enough evidence to prove the charge, and told the jury to return a verdict of not guilty. With that, Thomas Newport was acquitted.

Perhaps Lydia was worn down by the drawn-out process. How had she fared with her neighbours since Sarah's acquittal, after details of her private life had been flung into the public arena? Was she embarrassed having to go over her sexual interlude with Thomas Newport now that she was married? And if Thomas had been interfering with witnesses during the inquests, could he have put pressure on Lydia before the trial?

The attempted poisoning at Tollesbury

Once Thomas Newport had left the dock, 24-year-old Emma Elizabeth Hume of Tollesbury was tried for the attempted murder of her husband.

She had been examined at Witham Petty Session in April 1847, and, 'as some of the features of this case resembled that for which Catherine Foster suffered at Bury, the greatest anxiety was evinced to hear the proceedings, the room in which they took place being crowded by the inhabitants.'

Emma Elizabeth Playle married Thomas Hume, a widower, in 1840: she was only just eighteen, and he was fifty-one. At the Witham Petty Sessions 'their appearance and the great disparity between their ages created much astonishment,' but the *Essex Standard* exaggerated when it reported that Emma was 'in her 24th year, while her husband, who was dressed in the garb of a labourer and seemed excessively weak, is old enough to be her grandfather, being fast verging upon his seventieth year.' At trial, Emma was described as 'a decent looking female … neatly clad. The husband bore a very sickly appearance.'

Despite the seriousness of the charge, no counsel was engaged on either side, so a barrister had to fill in for the prosecution. Emma stood trial without any defence counsel.

Thomas Hume had been suffering from a liver complaint and had been taking pills to alleviate it. Emma brought him 'two large pills, which she took out of the box where the other pills were kept'. Thomas protested that they were too large and too strong, and refused to take them. He was suspicious – two weeks before, Emma had fried some potatoes for him. 'There was something in the taste that I could not eat them; it was a very nasty taste, and I could not swallow a bit; I spit the piece out of my mouth.'

After the potatoes, Emma prepared a broth for her husband, which he could not eat either. 'It was different to any broth I had taken before; it had a comical sweet taste.'

Emma interjected from the dock. She had been in the workhouse, and claimed that when she came out, Thomas had said he would put her to Chelmsford, even if he had to take a false oath.

'I knew you had enough money to keep me, and I thought it hard to be in the workhouse.'

Thomas denied it.

The next witness was the wife of Thomas's son; the four Humes shared the same house. She alleged that she had seen Emma making some pills with flour and water, which she laid on the stove to dry, then put in the box with Thomas's other pills. His son said that 'there were a good many brown pills, and two great white ones.' He was suspicious and passed them to the police: they were analysed and were found to contain twenty-six grains (1,685mg) of sugar of lead.

The judge summed up, commenting that the case had 'been got up in a manner not creditable to the county. Here is a serious charge against the prisoner intended to be prosecuted without the assistance of Counsel – without any attorney to get up the case.' He felt that much evidence had been omitted and blamed the county for trying to save money, exercising 'its economy too closely in leaving a case like this so bare of evidence and all professional assistance'.

The jury quickly returned a verdict of guilty. The judge felt the crime was so horrible that it was 'his duty to pass the most extreme sentence allowed by law, which was that she should be transported beyond the seas for the term of her natural life.' Poisoning with intent to kill was not a capital offence.

Emma had listened to the judge with composure, but once he passed sentence she 'rushed to the side of the dock against which her husband had been leaning, and made a violent effort to attack him.' She clung desperately onto the iron spikes of the dock, and it took three attendants to drag her away. Down she was taken to the prison van, where 'she became subdued, and vented her feelings in tears.'

A petition was got up by the people of Tollesbury to protest her sentence – under the Offences Against the Person Act, the punishment for administering poison was imprisonment or, in a particularly bad case, transportation. Before the Appeal Court was formed in 1875, a petition was one way to secure a change in sentencing. Even her husband added his mark to the petition, but to no avail: Emma's sentence was not commuted.

If only she had not been so impatient and had anticipated the inevitable outcome of her husband's illness. While she waited in prison for the ship that would take her away forever from her Essex marshland home to the other side of the world, Thomas Hume died.

In early 1848, Emma set sail for Van Diemen's Land on a convict ship; a few months later another poisoning was discovered in Essex.

Map of the Tendring Hundred and surrounding area mentioned in this book.

Chapter 2

'It's not a pleasant thought neither – is it? – to be buried like a pauper'

Inspector Samuel Raison of the Essex Constabulary usually dealt with the small crimes of village life. He had joined the Constabulary at its creation in 1840, and was promoted to inspector in 1846. Stationed in the Tendring Hundred, he dealt with such outrages as a drunk landlord in a Wivenhoe pub, meat stolen from a cart in Tendring, and the theft of a hat in Thorpe-le-Soken. But in June 1848, Reverend Wilkins, rector of Wix, asked him to investigate a suspicious death in his village.

While Clavering is so far to the north-west of Essex that it's almost in Hertfordshire and Cambridgeshire, the Tendring Hundred is so far to the north-east of Essex that it's almost in Suffolk and the North Sea. A peninsular, to the north it is bounded by the river Stour; to the south by the river Colne; to the east by the vast expanse of the North Sea and to

Wix parish church. The thirteenth-century arches can be seen along the wall.

the west, the ancient town of Colchester and the Dedham Vale. A largely rural area, it is in places flat by the coast with salt marshes, popular with smugglers, and there were oyster fisheries on the Colne at Brightlingsea. There are cliffs at Clacton, and the beaches along the coast would later make it a place for holidays. In the early twentieth century, Frinton would become a seaside resort for royalty, but in 1841 it was a tiny village, with a population of only forty-four people. Harwich, a port town to the extreme north-east of the peninsular, had had a Royal Naval Dockyard, and seventeenth-century diarist Samuel Pepys had been its MP. Inland are its farming villages, and agriculture is still a feature of the economy today, even though Ramsey's windmill no longer grinds any corn.

In 1581, ten women from St Osyth were convicted of witchcraft, and the witch-hunts during the Civil War in the 1640s, under the auspices of Matthew Hopkins, the 'witchfinder general', began in the Tendring Hundred. By the early eighteenth century, Protestant refugees from France and Belgium were settling in the area and established a Huguenot church in Thorpe-le-Soken. In 1803, with the threat of Napoleonic invasion on this vulnerable North Sea coast, a military camp was established at Weeley, home to thousands of Scottish soldiers and their families.

Until the construction of a bypass, the main road through the village of Wix was also a major route to Harwich, 6 miles to the east. In 1841, it had a population of just over 800 people. There were public houses and by 1847, Wix had a National School. Its church, a little way out of the village, has arches visible on the outer north wall, all that remains of the thirteenth-century chapel of the priory that once stood there. Wix Abbey, which stands beside it, is a misnomer – it is a late Elizabethan house built in red brick by William Vesey, a relative of Sir Thomas Bowes, who, as Justice of the Peace, helped Matthew Hopkins send many 'witches' to Chelmsford. Vesey's mother, Joan Suckling, an ancestor of Horatio Nelson, is buried in Wix's churchyard.

The unfortunate family of Mary May

Mary May's parents, James Angier (also spelt Anger or Ainger) and Mary Constable, married at Wix on 7 June 1808. Mary Constable had given birth to an illegitimate son called William some years earlier – he was known as both

William Constable and, using his natural father's surname, Spratty Watts. The baptisms for Mary and her half-brother have not come to light, and this inability to prove their ages would impact on what would happen later.

In 1819, William had an illegitimate child by Frances Sallas; a few months later they were married at Great Oakley. Three more children were born to them, but they don't appear to have survived childhood, and after Frances's death in 1823, it seems that William did not marry again.

As Mary Ainger, in 1825 Mary May married her first husband in Ramsey, 3½ miles north-east of Wix. If Mary had been born soon after her parents' marriage in 1808, then she was a young bride, being only about seventeen. Ramsey's baptism register shows six children of James Everett and Mary, most of whom died in infancy, and James himself died in 1840, aged thirty-six. As tragic as this is, it was by no means unusual at this period for a family to lose so many members in so short a time. At least the surviving children still had one remaining parent: now a widow with two young children, Mary left Ramsey. By the time of the 1841 census, she was living in Wix.

Reverend George Wilkins, Wix's rector at the time, would later claim in a letter to the *Essex Standard* that Mary and Robert May had lived together

Great Oakley parish church.

unmarried, and that he 'several times called upon them to induce them to be married. They at length consented, but said they had no money to pay the expenses.' So Wilkins married them without fees, on 5 November 1841. But were they really cohabiting? Any Victorian reading this letter would have felt that Mary was of dubious morals, and that her criminality was part and parcel of such. But the 1841 census, taken on the night of 6 June that year, shows Mary living alone with her two children; Robert was living with his brother and his family. Wilkins said that after Mary and Robert's marriage, 'a nice little girl of hers died suddenly and rather mysteriously' – but in fact, her daughter died over a month before the marriage.

Two children were born to Robert and Mary May – Jemima in about 1845, and William in about 1847. By 1848 their household consisted of two parents, two or three children, and two lodgers: Mary's half-brother, William, and another man called James Simpson. William carried on a variety of jobs – he appears to have been a day labourer on the farms as well as a dealer; he is referred to in some sources as a pedlar. Robert was an agricultural labourer, and Mary sold bread: they tried to get by any way they could.

Early in 1848, William was arrested by Inspector Raison, who thought he had stolen some metal from Reverend Wilkins. In April he was brought before the County Sessions: William Watts, aged forty-eight, a dealer in marine stores. He claimed that he hadn't realised the iron had been stolen, and pinned it on the prisoner who had been found guilty of larceny in the hearing before him. William was acquitted.

Marriage certificate of Robert May and Mary Everett.

Burial clubs

About a month after William's brush with the law, Mary was talking with her neighbour, Susannah Forster. Susannah was the mistress of Wix's National School – the one-storey redbrick building still stands today, now a private house on the road through Wix. A report in 1847, which may refer to Susannah, said: 'This school has suffered from repeated change of teachers, but it is carefully superintended by the clergyman and well supplied with apparatus. The mistress requires training. Funds raised with difficulty.'

Susannah, herself originally from Harwich, had entered her own brother in the New Mourner's Friend Society there, which would pay about £9 or £10 on her brother's death. This was not a small amount of money – it was about half what an agricultural labour could expect to earn in a year. When Susannah told Mary this, her neighbour decided that she would enter her brother in the club too.

Burial clubs and friendly societies were examples of working and lower middle-class Victorians self-organising; forming their own insurance clubs where members would pay in small amounts of money. A burial club would pay a sum of money on the death of a member to cover the cost of a funeral, and a friendly society would cover members for a certain period if they found themselves unable to work. Even the poorest members of Victorian society felt the stigma of a pauper's burial. A report in the *Morning Chronicle* in 1850 wrote how elderly inmates of workhouses spoke with emotion at the thought of being buried 'by the parish': 'Pointing to a small enclosed spot, which the small green mounds marked as the paupers' burial-ground [they said] – "There will be my home at last, and it's not a pleasant thought neither – is it? – to be buried like a pauper."'

Another reason to avoid a pauper burial was that, following the 1832 Anatomy Act, they could end up on the dissection slab. Before this date, only the corpses of executed criminals could be used by anatomy students and scientists, and in order to satisfy demand the 'resurrection men' took to digging up graves or, in the case of Burke and Hare, turned to murder. The number of capital offences in Britain was decreasing in the 1830s, so to put the resurrection men out of business, a plentiful supply of bodies was required. This was amply furnished by the corpses of the poor. Following the Act, any corpse destined for a pauper burial could be sold by parish authorities to anatomical teaching schools. Whilst some people were happy to donate their body for dissection, for others it went against their religious beliefs: a dissected corpse could not rise from the grave whole on Judgment Day.

Avoiding this undignified end was difficult as funerals were not cheap: the *Morning Chronicle* found that an agricultural labourer could be expected to pay at least £4 10s. They discovered that funeral costs were inflated in Harwich because they were 'three-deep' – not a reference to the number of people in a single grave plot, but the number of middlemen involved in conducting the funeral. It is possible that this same unnecessarily high price was a factor in surrounding villages such as Wix.

On top of the price of the funeral was the cost of mourning clothes. Mourning had become codified, with rules about what could and couldn't be worn by whom, depending on who had died and how long ago; it was a huge industry in the Victorian period. Demand was such that in 1841, Jay's London General Mourning Warehouse opened on Regent Street, to cater for the affluent, but for everyone else, local sempstresses would run up mourning clothes. While the strict rules of full- and half-mourning were perhaps not followed by ordinary Victorians, even on a limited budget they would try to make some observance. So while a fairly basic funeral could cost about £5 or £6, there were added expenses in kitting out a family in respectable mourning wear.

By the late 1840s, friendly societies and burial clubs were falling out of favour with the establishment. In 1845, Sarah Freeman of Shapwick, Somerset, was accused of murdering her brother, who was in a burial club; the sudden deaths of her other relatives were investigated and she was executed. The following year, John Rodda was hanged at York Castle, convicted of having murdered his infant son with oil of vitriol (sulphuric acid), apparently to receive a payment of fifty shillings (less than £3) from the burial club in which the child had been entered. By October that year, a Bill was passing through Parliament to regulate friendly societies, and *The Times* criticised the British fondness for signing up to clubs:

There are very few labourers who do not belong to at least one club. The more provident out of the humblest weekly pittance will sometimes subscribe to a friendly club comprehending relief both to age and sickness, a medical club, a burial club, and clothing club, and, perhaps to one or two other objects.

The Times felt that these endeavours, including building societies where labourers could save up and eventually buy their own property, were 'generally abortive', stating there were innumerable examples of clubs and societies going bankrupt and being open to fraud and quarrels, as well as members being denied relief when they made a claim. *The Times* blamed the mania for societies and clubs on the fact that 'there is a remarkable and a lamentable deficiency of opportunities available for the advancement of the poor,' tying the idea up with nineteenth-century paternalism. The poor should be helped to advance, but not left to do it themselves.

Only ten years before, the Tolpuddle Martyrs – who had formed a union in order to protect the wages of agricultural labourers – had been sentenced to transportation. Although trade unions were no longer illegal, an obscure law about oath-swearing was invoked, for which they were prosecuted. It was an example of how self-organising workers threatened and unnerved the establishment, as Britain looked on at the revolutions in Europe.

As part of his investigation into the sanitary condition of towns in 1843, Edwin Chadwick investigated burials and burial clubs. He pointed out that people joined multiple clubs for fear that they were not financially secure – a club might go under and take any chance of a decent burial with it. Writing before Freeman and Rodda's crimes, Chadwick suspected that burial clubs were being misused, and that entering someone – specifically a child – in multiple clubs, even for fear of the club failing, placed 'a bounty on neglect and infanticide'. He quoted a minister in Manchester who observed too much levity at funerals, and he was shocked 'by a common phrase amongst women of the lowest class – "Aye, aye, that child will not live; it is in the burial club."'

Chadwick cited the case of a child who had been entered into ten clubs and was apparently starved to death, her parents receiving £35. In total, they had received another £20 from the deaths of six other children who lived from only nine to eighteen months. Chadwick mentions two other cases – in one, the parents were found guilty of poisoning their children with arsenic; all of them had been entered into burial clubs.

Was it really the case that people, on a grand scale, were entering their children in multiple burial clubs merely to kill them and make off with the money? Or was it that because so many people entered family members in burial clubs, the chances were that somewhere in that number were a tiny fraction who were willing to commit murder?

On 13 May 1848, Mary May and Susannah Forster made the 6-mile journey to Harwich. They met John Pratt, a shoemaker, who was the club's collector. As the club wasn't full, Susannah told him that Mary wished to become a member, and to nominate her brother, William Constable. The clubs had rules about the health and the age of their members – with child mortality high, some clubs would not enrol children, and most had an upper age limit; neither would they enter people who were already ailing.

John asked Mary how old she was, and she replied that she was twenty-nine. He wasn't convinced and asked her if she was older – she insisted that she wasn't. She said she was in good health, and that her brother was a strong, healthy man, who was not more than thirty-five years old. John asked Susannah to corroborate this, and she said, 'I saw him in the hay field this morning: he is a hearty strong man, and not more than thirty-five.'

John said, 'You must not be surprised at my asking these pointed questions, as I am subject to a fine if I do not put them, and if people give improper answers, they deceive themselves and get no benefit from the club.'

He later claimed that, because he didn't know Mary, he wouldn't have entered William without seeing him first if it hadn't been for Susannah's statement.

Spratty Watts falls ill

William Constable was seen out in the fields working on Wednesday, 7 June. He was in his usual health, although he wasn't a strong man and was usually ailing. In the early afternoon of Thursday, William went off to Tendring, a village just south of Wix, with his nephew to fetch some sheep for George Low. George was the landlord of the White Hart public house, and also worked as a butcher. Even today, an iron ring can be seen on one of the floor beams of the pub, where the animals were tethered for slaughtering. Avice, George's wife, gave William some bullock's liver and suet as payment, which William had requested in lieu of cash.

When James Simpson returned home that evening, he found William sitting by the fire; he looked ill and complained of stomach pains. Mary had been to see her neighbour, Mary Feint, saying that her brother looked so bad, she thought he would die. Feint visited and said, 'Watts, you look very bad.'

'Yes, I am,' he replied. He said he had a bad pain across his body and in his head, and that he felt sick.

From 'The Hours of the Night', *Illustrated Exhibitor & Magazine of Art*, 1852.

James followed him into the yard, where he saw William 'standing against the pales very sick.' William went up to bed, and called down to James – he had vomited. Mary was out of the house at the time, and once James himself had gone to bed, she came in and sat with her brother for about fifteen minutes, and held the chamber pot for him as he retched.

At about four o'clock on Friday morning, James called Mary in to help; William was afflicted with vomiting and diarrhoea. James left for work. Although it was early, the long daylight hours of June kept agricultural labourers busy with hay-making.

Mary Feint visited again that morning, and William told her that he still felt ill, but should shortly be better. Mary May didn't share his optimism, and told her neighbour that William had asked if Mary Feint would lay him out after his death.

That evening, Robert May went to Manningtree, about 6 miles from Wix; he had an order from the relieving officer for the surgeon, William Thompson. It was a long trip, presumably made on foot – the relieving officer lived about 7 miles from Wix, and then he had to travel further still to reach the surgeon. Thompson worked over six parishes, about 11,000 acres, as well as being responsible for the many unfortunates in the Tendring Union House. He was out when Robert arrived. Martin Perry, Thompson's assistant, asked for the patient's symptoms. With Thompson unavailable, and deciding not to make a visit, Perry sent Robert away with two medicines. One was powdered rhubarb, and the other was a mixture of catechu (an extract from the acacia tree), opium, ginger, chalk and water. Rhubarb has several uses in medicine, one of which is a purgative; catechu is used for treating diarrhoea; ginger is traditionally used for gastric problems and can reduce nausea; opium would provide pain relief; chalk, like milk of magnesia, would settle an upset stomach. William had been prescribed medicine that would purge him as well as soothe his irritated insides.

While Robert was out, James sat up until midnight talking to Mary May. She took the opportunity of her husband's absence to tell her lodger about the burial club, but that her husband did not know. When later giving testimony, James couldn't be sure if she had said that William didn't know himself either. Mary told James that 'if she got the money she would bury him respectably and have some mourning for him.' She also said that with any money left over, 'she meant to buy a cart and go about the country higgling [peddling].'

News of William's illness had spread about the village. On Saturday, 10 June, Charlotte Elvish, another relative of this author, called to visit him. Charlotte was the wife of a journeyman wheelwright, who had known William some time; she first moved to the area ten years before. She held her friend's head as he vomited, and said to Mary that he was clearly very ill. She expressed surprise at how swiftly his health had deteriorated. Charlotte had seen William, as had many others, at work in the fields only a couple of days earlier, but Mary insisted that he'd been ill for several days.

That same day at noon, William Thompson visited the patient, who told him that 'he was considerably better than he had been the evening before,' thanks to the medicine that Perry had prepared for him. Although the surgeon did not think William was in immediate danger, he considered him too ill to remove to the workhouse infirmary. Thompson ordered some mutton broth for him and to send for more medicine in the morning.

On Sunday, 11 June, William told James that Inspector Raison had hit him over the head, and that was what was killing him. Mary fetched Susannah Forster, who found William 'in bed, and his son sat by his side'. She spoke to him, but William was by now so weak that he could not reply other than by shaking his head. Susannah left and went to church, and on her return, heard that William had died.

Mary, illiterate so unable to do so herself, asked Susannah to write a letter to the New Mourners' Friend Society, and to specify in it that she had seen William shortly before his death:

> Wix, Sunday noon, June 11th
>
> Sir – I have to record the death of my brother, William Constable, which took place at a quarter-past twelve this day. He was taken with strong inflammation. Doctor Thompson, of Manningtree, attended him. He was at work in the hay field on Tuesday last, when he was taken with a pain in the head and sickness. Susannah Forster saw him a short time before he died.
>
> Your's respectfully,
> Mrs May

Robert May took the letter to Harwich, and John Raison, a smack owner who was also the burial club's secretary, gave him a note to give the undertaker that would guarantee the funeral expenses.

On Monday, Mary May asked Mary Feint if she would register the death. She told her to enter his age as thirty-eight, saying it was the closest she could get from him. This seems unlikely given that when William was arrested a few months before, the newspaper says he was forty-eight; presumably he volunteered his age himself. Mary Feint quibbled: she was about fifty, and she had known William for about forty-five years. She believed he was slightly younger than herself, and even her father thought as much too. But Mary May insisted that it should be thirty-eight, so this is the age that went on the certificate.

Having laid out William, Mary Feint headed to Manningtree. Although Thompson's assistant offered a certificate if the registrar required, he did not ask for one, and the cause of death was incorrectly recorded as 'decline, lasting three months'. Mary May hadn't given a description of what had killed William, so the cause of death might have been supplied by Mary Feint or the registrar had settled on it in lieu of other information.

Reverend Wilkins: amateur sleuth

It was mid-June, the weather hot and stormy. There were reports of hayrick fires, not the result of arson by discontented farm workers, but caused by lightning striking the tinder-dry hay. Reverend Wilkins heard about William's death on the day he died, and a day or so later Mary May went to see him about arranging the funeral. She said that William needed to be buried as soon as possible 'as he was a very bad corpse.' It would not have been pleasant to have a body in their cramped cottage in warm weather.

William received a pauper's burial on Wednesday, 14 June. Reverend Wilkins asked Mary what her brother's real name was – he had always known him as Spratty Watts. Mary said that his actual name was William Constable. The parish register entry says 'William Constable' with an asterisk directing attention to the bottom of the page, where Wilkins added, 'This man was better known by an alias, Spratty Watts.'

A box tomb in Wix churchyard. William Constable's pauper resting place would have had a wooden marker, if anything at all.

He asked Mary for her brother's age, and once again, she said that he had been thirty-eight. Wilkins said he thought he was older than that, but Mary insisted, even when Wilkins suggested that she meant forty-eight instead.

She said, 'No, thirty-eight, I must know, for I am but twenty-nine.'

Wilkins gave her a certificate of the burial, at her request. Nearly two weeks later, on 26 June, Mary called on Wilkins again, asking for a favour. She told him that she needed a certificate from him stating that her brother had been in good health a fortnight before his death. Wilkins refused, telling her she must go to the doctor for one. She pressed him, saying others would corroborate he had been well. Wilkins asked what she required it for, so Mary showed him a letter from the secretary of the burial club. They refused to pay out unless Mary gave good evidence that her brother was healthy at the time she had signed him up.

'But this money does not belong to you,' Wilkins said. 'It belongs to your husband.'

His response reflected the relative powerlessness of women at the time – until the Married Women's Property Act of 1870, money that came to a woman as a wage, an investment, a gift or inheritance was automatically that of her husband. This would have included insurance payouts, as in the case of a burial club.

Mary replied, 'He's got a son.'

Wilkins' riposte was, 'He's illegitimate and cannot inherit it.'

Even today in Britain, an illegitimate child cannot inherit their parents' property without being named in a will; this predicament inspired Wilkie Collins's 1862 novel *No Name*.

Wilkins repeated that the burial club money would have to belong to Mary's husband, but she said, 'My husband knows nothing about it – I put him in the club myself.'

Wilkins insisted that, because William had been buried by the parish, it was the parish itself that had a claim to the money. What had become of the note given to Robert May by the burial club's secretary, to guarantee the expenses of William's funeral?

Wilkins decided it was time to involve Inspector Raison. The policeman visited Mary, and after confirming that she had entered her brother in the burial club, he said to her, 'I understand that you can't get the money.'

Raison offered to investigate for her, asking Mary to tell him about William's health. She told him that William drove some sheep on the day he fell ill, and that she gave him ginger beer and a biscuit as he set off. Raison asked if the ginger beer had been sour and turned his stomach, but Mary said, 'No, that it wasn't, for he wasn't sick, and that my neighbour knows.' She continually denied to Raison that her brother had vomited at all. Presumably thinking he could convince the burial club that William hadn't been ill, she said, 'Yes, and you'll put it down on that paper that you consider he was in his usual health at the time he was taken.' She added, 'Poor old soul, I miss him everywhere, for he never gave me an angry word in his life, and my neighbour, Mrs Feint, knows.'

Raison said he would go and speak to Mrs Feint, but Mary immediately rose from her chair, and said she would fetch her.

'Oh no,' Raison replied, 'I'll go myself, and then the club will think there's no smuggling in it.'

It is interesting that 'smuggling' was a slang term for underhand behaviour at this time, reflecting how common that illegal activity was along the Essex coast.

Mrs Feint told the inspector that she thought William had been well, too, and on returning to Mary with this news, Raison asked her again, 'Then you are sure, Mrs May, he was not sick at all?'

'On no, that he was not.'

She told Raison about some beer she had served up for her brother on 8 June, when he complained of feeling ill – that she had boiled it up with an egg and put some nutmeg in it. Raison asked Mary if she had bought anything from Harwich when she'd gone to sign her brother up.

'As the club people say he was not well at the time you entered him, did you get any powders or pills for him?'

'Oh Lor', Mr Raison,' Mary replied, 'You think I got something and gave him, and killed him, I know that's what you think. Poor old soul, I never hurt a hair on his head, he was the only friend I had in the world.'

Wilkins and Raison went to Harwich to find out more about the burial club and the circumstances under which Mary had entered her brother. It seems like something from *The Grantchester Mysteries* or *Father Dowling Investigates* – the local vicar teaming up with a police inspector, but Wilkins's involvement is explained by the pastoral role a minister has in their local community. Wilkins was keenly engaged in many aspects of village life – when he died in 1877 after serving Wix as its vicar for forty years, the *Essex Standard*'s obituary quoted at length from the *Gardeners' Chronicle*, which had included him in a section on 'Noteworthy Agriculturalists'. They remembered him as 'one of our agricultural heroes' who took an active interest in rural life and had 'a sense of duty to his neighbour'; he frequently wrote to both publications with his views on rural and farming matters. Even while the investigation into William Constable's death went on, Wilkins was personally examining potato crops in Essex, Kent, Surrey and Sussex for signs of potato blight. His energetic involvement with Mary May's case, which he seems to have engaged with on a personal and emotional level, confirms the *Essex Standard's* view of him as a 'somewhat eccentric clergyman'.

Charles Tweed was a baker who lived at Bradfield, about 2 miles north-west of Wix. He would later claim that on 28 June Mary had approached him, saying, 'Charley, I've got into a muddle, and I want you to help me out. It is not money I want, but they say old Watts has been poisoned, and they are going to take up his body.'

The Waggon in Wix, still serving beers but no longer hosting coroners' inquests.

She asked Tweed to say that he had seen her brother drink from a bottle in a field, and hadn't been well since. Tweed was reluctant, but Mary had said, 'Pray do, for the sake of my poor children; for if anything happens that will clear me.'

So Tweed did as Mary had asked, and spread the story at public houses around Wix.

On 29 June, Raison arrived again at the May's cottage with Constable Emson, and told Mary there was to be an inquest into her brother's death as there was suspicion surrounding it. He asked her to attend, and Mary said, 'Oh, he told me, he found a bottle as he was going up a field and drank out of it, and had never been well since, and if there's anything found in him, I didn't give it him.' She added, in a low voice, 'As true as God, child, he would have hung himself one day not long ago if it hadn't been for me; he took a line, went up in the field, and I ran after him.'

Raison asked her how long ago that had happened, and she answered, 'Two months. I wish he had hung himself, and if I'd known I was going to get into this trouble I would have let him.'

Inquest

The inquest into the death of William Constable, aka Spratty Watts, opened at the Waggon public house in Wix on Friday, 30 June. His body had been exhumed from the churchyard that morning and the coroner, William Codd, came up from his home in Maldon to investigate.

Whereas the Clavering and Manuden inquests had dragged on for months, the Wix inquest was over in just one week. At the first meeting, Mary Feint spoke, outlining William's illness and the relationship he had with his sister. The lodger, James Simpson, was threatened with imprisonment by Codd, who was aware that what James said differed from statements he had given the police.

He asked, 'Has Mrs May told you not to say anything about this matter?' James said she had only told him to tell the truth.

Mary was brought in. She did not have any legal representation, and having had the depositions read over to her, she agreed with them and did not question the witnesses.

Next to speak was William Thompson, the Manningtree surgeon, who discussed his patient's symptoms and what he had found during the post-mortem carried out that morning. Allowing for decomposition, all he could say was that William's insides showed no ill health apart from some red patches that indicated inflammation. He could not analyse this further himself.

The meeting was adjourned after five hours. Although other witnesses were waiting to be examined, Codd decided they could go no further without Professor Taylor's analysis.

John Bird, another Manningtree surgeon, who had assisted with the post-mortem, took the viscera to London on Saturday. Professor Taylor began his analysis at once, in Bird's presence. He saw the telltale streak of yellow in the stomach, which indicated white arsenic trioxide that had turned into arsenic trisulfide; using the Reinsch test, he found the poison present. He separately boiled part of the stomach and the duodenum, and found arsenic in both.

Taylor wrote his report on Monday, 3 July, and with forensic evidence proving that William had died of arsenic poisoning, Mary May was arrested at once.

The investigation was resumed at the Waggon inn on 4 July, 'but the apartment soon became so crowded that it was found necessary to adjourn to the parish schoolroom, the use of which was offered by the Incumbent.' Once again, we see the hand of Reverend Wilkins. The news of Taylor's results 'manifestly increased the excitement prevailing in the neighbourhood' and as the schoolroom was so crowded, 'a large number of the labouring population who could not gain admittance thronged round the windows to obtain a peep at the interior.' Mary May was present: the prime reason for the locals pressing their noses up against the glass.

After Codd had read out Taylor's report – printed in full scientific and anatomical detail by the *Essex Standard* – Wilkins gave his evidence, telling the coroner and the jury about Mary approaching him for help. Mary, once again without legal counsel, questioned him – was he positive that she had told him her husband knew nothing about William being entered in the burial club? Wilkins replied that he was.

John Pratt from the New Mourners' Friend Society was questioned, and the club's secretary showed the letter written on the day of William's death.

William Rayner, the registrar, gave evidence about Mary Feint registering William's death, and she was brought in once again. The coroner believed that 'she knew a great more about this affair than she was willing to state.' Perhaps mindful of the threats of imprisonment received by James Simpson at the first meeting, Mary Feint went into more detail, and talked about the discrepancy of William's age.

Charlotte Elvish gave her sickroom evidence, and James Simpson spoke again. Unlike his brief testimony at the first meeting, he gave a fuller version – as Codd did not threaten him with imprisonment this time, James presumably gave an account that was closer to the one he had given the police before.

Avice Low talked about William droving the sheep for her husband, and then Susannah Forster spoke. Perhaps feeling the strangeness of her school turning into a coroner's court, she talked about registering William in the burial club and what happened in the sickroom. She also added that, 'Since the first inquest Mrs May has told me about his taking a rope to hang himself; and also that he had drank from a bottle which he found and had not been well since; I never heard either story before, although I have been in the habit of seeing her daily since 1 May.'

Mary had arrived in the schoolroom evincing 'the greatest indifference and unconcern'. However, while Avice and Susannah gave evidence, her 'countenance and manner changed considerably.' The *Essex Standard* reported that Mary was an 'artful looking woman' but something that was said by the two women unsettled her. It was clear to all concerned that Mary's stories about the rope and the bottle weren't true and had been concocted to hide something. And that something, it was believed, was the poisoning of her own brother.

The inquest was adjourned, it being by then ten o'clock at night. When the *Essex Standard* reported the two inquest meetings, they printed something that would be repeated across the country whenever May's case was reported:

> Some suspicion begins to be entertained as to former proceedings of the prisoner, who is known to have buried fourteen out of sixteen children, and it is said one or two of the latest deaths (about six years ago), as also that of her first husband, took place rather suddenly.

Comparing parish baptism and burial registers shows that infant mortality was a problem even in a rural district like the Tendring Hundred, which would have seen a higher life expectancy than in large towns. Mary and her first husband had six children baptised; only one was still alive by 1848. Could it be that 'six children' had been misheard, and the circus of gossip and excitement had turned that number into sixteen?

Other than by routinely giving birth to twins and triplets, it is almost impossible for one woman to have had that many children. None of the baptisms for Mary's children were for multiple births, and from the general picture that can be gained from parish registers, it also seems that a woman having one birth per year was unusual. It is more the case that a couple would have one child once every two or three years, partly due to breastfeeding having a contraceptive effect, and because poor nutrition and ill health of either parent can negatively affect fertility. The gaps we see in the register between baptisms of Mary's children (the largest being just over four years between Eliza at the end of 1831 and Alfred at the beginning of 1836) could be explained, not by unregistered, murdered children, but by her having lost children through miscarriages.

At least one of the Everett children had been baptised privately, as was Jemima May. This was usually done at home, sometimes by a midwife rather than a minister, when a child was weak at birth and it was thought they would not survive to Sunday service when they would be publicly baptised. The rite was clearly important to Mary, so it seems unlikely that there were other children who were not baptised, unless they died too soon after birth for even a private baptism. There are no unbaptised children of Mary mentioned in the burial register, although the vicar might have made a practice of not recording them.

But consider that William's death looked like a burial club murder, and consider that Chadwick's research showed that children were the usual victims. As other writers have pointed out, the idea of Mary having murdered her own children would put her in step with those other burial club murders. Yet there was no evidence she had entered anyone other than her brother into a burial club: no motive was ever suggested for those other alleged murders.

At the final meeting of the inquest, on Friday, 7 July, Professor Taylor gave evidence. He would have come up from London on the train to Manningtree Station, which was then the nearest station to Wix. It isn't clear if this final meeting took place in the Waggon inn or the schoolroom, but once more, Professor Taylor found himself the toxicological expert in an Essex village, proving that arsenic had killed again.

'I have not the slightest doubt whatever,' Taylor told the crowd gathered in Wix, 'that death was caused by inflammation of the stomach, and that the inflammation was caused by the action of the arsenic.'

Martin Perry, the Manningtree surgeon's assistant, described the medicines he had given Robert May. He was careful to point out that there was no arsenic in the medicine, and that the only arsenic they had was kept on a different shelf from the ingredients in the medicine, so could not have crept in by accident.

Two more Wix locals gave evidence as to William's health, which would help to establish when he had fallen ill and therefore roughly when he consumed the arsenic. It all pointed to the arsenic taking effect in the late afternoon of 8 June.

While the money from the burial club was a clear motive for Mary to kill her brother, there had to be evidence that she had acquired and administered the poison. Mary Feint gave evidence for a third time, saying that thirteen or fourteen weeks before, about the time that William was accused of stealing from Reverend Wilkins, Mary May went to Manningtree to get some arsenic to poison the rats. Mary Feint had never seen rats in the Mays' cottage, but had seen what looked like rats' holes, and Mary May had said she spread the arsenic onto bread and butter and left it on the floor.

Mary Feint's 15-year-old daughter, also called Mary, went with May to Manningtree. May had bought herself a dress, and then had gone to the chemist's. Mary Feint junior stood by the door, where she heard May ask 'for some poison or arsenic, I cannot quite recollect which.' The chemist asked what it was for, and May replied that it was for killing the rats, 'for they ran over her bed at night.' He offered something else for 6d that would do as well, but, according to Mary Feint junior, she said, 'No, I can't give so much' – arsenic would have been cheaper, but Mary Feint junior did not see Mary buy anything, and they left.

The chemist himself gave evidence. Mary May had not been in his shop for about four months, although she had been a regular customer for some time. He said, 'I cannot recollect having ever served her with arsenic, but if she had applied for it I should have given it to her without hesitation, from having known her so long.'

Neither could he corroborate what Mary Feint junior had said about offering something else for killing the rats. However, a packet of Butler's Rat Poison was produced, which Mary May identified. It was a brown powder whose base was white arsenic.

Inspector Raison gave evidence at length, explaining what Mary May had said to him as he went about his investigations. He had searched her house for arsenic and not found any, and he claimed that Mary had said to him, 'I never had any poison in the house in my life, I don't know what he had – if he had anything he took it himself, for I never gave it to him.' She claimed the locals were against her and that if they had known Raison was searching her house, they would have put some poison in her cottage to incriminate her. Raison quoted her as having said, 'You should have asked some of them old shepherds and rat-catchers, for Watts used to be about along with they; for he used to have stuff for his sheep and say it was poison, but what sort I don't know.'

Unfortunately for Mary, the fact that she had entered her brother into a burial club without his knowledge seemed so suspicious that it overrode any attempt to demonstrate how he might have been poisoned by accident. It's worth recalling that just before James and Joseph Chesham died of arsenic poisoning in Clavering, their brother Philip had been out droving sheep himself. As arsenic was used in sheep dip, it could suggest how these deaths came about. If it really had been the case that William had somehow ingested arsenic by accident through working with sheep, that fact was lost in the desperate lies Mary burbled, trying to save herself.

Gossip was rife. Mary Feint senior reported a conversation she had had with Mary on the morning that William was exhumed – only hours before the inquest was opened.

Apparently, Mary May had said, 'It's all through lies that I am brought to this trouble, for the police have been to me two or three times about Watts's death.'

Feint commented, 'Do you know the tale there is abroad, they even say they know where you bought the poison?'

'Why really, neighbour,' Mary May retorted, 'You think I done the deed.'

Of course there would be gossip flying about Wix and nearby villages, and Raison reported Mary as having said, 'Oh dear me, it's hard to suffer innocently, and everybody is telling lies about me and trying to hang me.'

The coroner asked Mary if she had anything to say.

'All I've got to say is, I never done the crime, and I don't know who did. I never gave him anything in my life only what I should not mind taking myself.'

He then summed up, and the jury took fifteen minutes to return the verdict of 'wilful murder' against Mary May.

The next day, she was sent to the old gaol in Chelmsford.

Trial at the Summer Assizes

The speed with which the law sometimes moved in the nineteenth century is quite astonishing to us now – William Constable had died on 8 June, and less than a month later, the inquest verdict returned wilful murder against his sister. Before the end of July, Mary May, ungallantly described by *The Times* as 'a repulsive-looking woman', was standing in the dock at Chelmsford Shire Hall.

Mary perhaps felt confident because her counsel, Charles Chadwick Jones, had successfully defended Sarah Chesham the year before. He had with him Thomas Chambers, who, ironically, prosecuted at Sarah's trial. They were assisted by George John Durrant, a young Chelmsford solicitor. Although Reverend Wilkins was convinced of Mary's guilt, it was he who engaged counsel for her at his own cost. When Jones and Chambers realised who had employed them, they 'generously refused to accept fees.' It isn't clear if Wilkins specifically chose Jones, but if he had, it could explain how Mary ended up with Sarah Chesham's defence counsel.

Prosecuting were Rodwell and Archer Ryland. The judge was Sir Frederick Pollock, who had twice been Attorney General, and at the time of Mary May's trial was Lord Chief Baron of the Exchequer. Once again, we find an ordinary woman from a small Essex village confronted by men who had no idea what it was like to live in a cramped, rat-infested cottage, or to be almost entirely powerless in Victorian society, by virtue of both class and sex.

Thirty-eight prisoners stood trial at these assizes, including Reason Field, a relative of this author. Field was accused of arson, and even though it was known he had a grudge against the person whose property he was seen leaving, and he had in his possession lucifer matches of a kind that were also found at the property, he was found not guilty. It is worth comparing to Mary May's case, because for both, evidence was circumstantial, and it wasn't the first time that Field had been accused of arson. Perhaps because the fire had not caused any loss of life, Field was given the benefit of the doubt.

Ryland opened the trial outlining the case for the prosecution, saying the charge was 'of the most appalling and horrifying kind'. He went through the facts of the case, placing emphasis on the fact that Mary had lied about

Henry William Field (1861–1941), the author's great–great–grandfather, with his wife Sarah, circa 1900–1910. Born in Brightlingsea with family across the Tendring Hundred, it is through Henry that I am related to several people who appear in this book. Reason Field was Henry's great-uncle.

her age and her brother's when entering him in the burial club, and had intentionally used a name by which he was not generally known. *The Times* inaccurately reported Ryland, underscoring Mary's mendacity by saying that she had entered him under a false name. Ryland highlighted how small an amount £10 was, as did Pollock when summing up. Of course, to men such as these, £10 truly was but a trifling amount – when Pollock died in 1870, he left about £45,000.

The same witnesses who had given evidence at the inquest in Wix, in the local pub and the village school, were now ushered into the wood-panelled grandeur of Shire Hall. There were, however, three extra witnesses.

William Butler briefly took the stand – he had manufactured Butler's Rat Powder, and Hooker, the Manningtree chemist, recommended it for anyone having trouble with rats. Butler explained that he had made it from May 1845 to September 1847, and that the basis of the powder was white arsenic.

The second new witness was Mary's oldest surviving child, William Everett. It is a horrible image, her 9-year-old son weeping 'bitterly during the delivery of his evidence', knowing that what he said could very well make him an orphan. He recalled going out with his uncle for the sheep, and that when he came back he fetched some porter for his mother. She boiled it in a saucepan with an egg 'and took something from a paper which she put into the porter, and after boiling it gave it to Watts.' This was the evidence needed to prove how Mary had administered the arsenic.

But under cross-examination, he said that his mother 'put soda into the porter and was in the habit of doing so when it was stale.' Was it really arsenic after all?

The third was Charles Tweed, the Bradfield baker. It seems his evidence only came to light after William Everett had been questioned after the inquest.

The reporting of the trial differs between the *Essex Standard* and the *Chelmsford Chronicle* – the *Essex Standard* only reported the speeches of the prosecution and defence, and then the judge's direction to the jury, saying that the witnesses' evidence 'was similar to that deposed at the inquest, fully reported at the time.' But this meant they missed out the crucial evidence of Mary's son. It may have been pressure of space that led to reporting the trial so briefly – both papers had to include a supplement in their issues for 28 July to carry all the extra columns generated by reports on the assize.

It isn't known how confident Serjeant Jones was as he defended Mary May, despite winning acquittals for Sarah Chesham. His closing speech, which the *Chelmsford Chronicle* commented was of 'considerable length' and *The Times* called 'a most earnest and eloquent appeal', mirrored that of the ones he had delivered during Sarah Chesham's trials. Just as he had claimed that Sarah had been a good, loving mother, attentive in the sickroom, without any motive to kill her sons, Jones now spoke in similar terms about Mary, that she was affectionate, kind and attentive to her brother, both before and during his illness:

> Look at her conduct from first to last – see whether it is the conduct of a sister – see whether it is the conduct of a Christian woman dealing with the parties in the house – and see if her conduct towards her brother is other than became her relationship to him.

He made some factual errors in his speech, which Ryland and Pollock corrected him on. Even if Jones had been engaged before the day of the trial, it happened so soon after the inquest, he would have had well under a month to prepare. The witnesses who gave evidence who didn't attend the inquests were something Jones had to digest on the day.

Whereas the prosecution claimed that killing for such a small sum showed how despicable Mary was, Jones turned it on its head. Using the same reasoning he had with Sarah Chesham – that it was so horrible for a woman to kill her own children that it was therefore unlikely to have happened – he claimed that killing for £10 was unthinkable and therefore couldn't be considered as the motive.

Ryland, in his speech, had pointed out that there was something shady in Mary's approach to the burial club; that her intention all along had been deception and murder. She had chosen a club in Harwich when there were others much nearer. Jones picked this argument apart by pointing out that Mary had only thought to register her brother when she heard Susannah Forster had entered her own brother in the Harwich club.

And to counter the issue of the inaccurate ages, Jones said, 'You know very well that there are numbers of persons in the agricultural districts who do not know their own ages.' Certainly anyone who has traced people through nineteenth-century censuses will have noticed this, where someone's age doesn't match up with the year of their birth (or estimated birth if there is only a baptism), and which can vary each time they appear on the census, and then varies again on their death certificate. This was not a huge proportion of the populace engaging in deception, but people who had been born before civil registration and were quite possibly illiterate anyway. The date of birth was rarely recorded in baptism registers, so many people, even if they still had their baptism certificate, would only have a vague idea of when they had been born.

He claimed that William could have been under forty-five, but that 'it may have been that the deceased had been in the early part of his life irregular and intemperate in his habits,' which would have aged his appearance. In fact, 'the probability is that the prisoner was no more correctly informed of his age than she was of her own.' Jones reminded the jury that Susannah Forster had corroborated Mary May's assertion of her brother's age.

And why, if he was so suspicious of the prisoner, had Reverend Wilkins accepted Mary's claim that her brother was thirty-eight when she went to bury him? 'The reverend gentleman might have made enquiries, but he did not, and the conclusion was, that he was satisfied it was the real age of the deceased.' Wilkins would still have been none the wiser – looking through all the parish and non-conformist registers for the Tendring Hundred for the period around William and Mary's supposed births has not yet yielded up their baptisms.

It is curious to note, however, that when Mary appeared on the 1841 census her age is given as thirty. Adults' ages on the 1841 census were rounded down, so a birth date of 1811 at the latest seems vaguely accurate, based on her parents' marriage in 1808 and her first marriage in 1825; the newspapers reporting the trial gave her age as thirty-eight, as does the criminal register of the assize. Did she volunteer the age of thirty, or did the census enumerator guess it from her appearance? If she had stated her age to be at least thirty in 1841, why, seven years later on entering her brother in the burial club, did she claim to be twenty-eight? Had she a very loose conception of age and numbers or is this extra evidence, which wasn't available at the time of her trial, that she really had knowingly deceived the burial club? Added to the fact that William's age was given as forty-eight when he was on trial himself earlier in 1848, Mary's claim that thirty-eight was the closest she could get out of him when asking, falls somewhat flat. Jones's defence, convincing as it is, is somewhat derailed by these facts. It would seem that Mary had lied to the burial club after all – but whether that was to shore up a burial for her brother should he need it or done with murder in mind, is something we might never know. The vanished note for the undertaker and William's swift pauper burial does not support Mary's innocence, but this was not remarked on in newspaper reports of her trial.

Jones continued, like the Essex wool-combers of old, to tease apart every aspect of the prosecution's case. He reasoned that: Inspector Raison had committed a wrong by claiming to help Mary when he was really there to investigate Reverend Wilkins's suspicions; the hot weather at the time of William's death would make a swift burial imperative 'not only for the sake of their comfort but their health' and was not due to a guilty person trying to conceal evidence of murder; and for Mary to admit at the inquest that she bought Butler's Rat Poison when no one else corroborated it was a sign of innocence because a guilty person would have used the lack of evidence from others to cover up the purchase. He also asked why, if she was guilty, she told James Simpson that she would spend some of the money on a horse and cart when that could be used as evidence against her.

He addressed the issue of her son's evidence, 'the little boy who had been brought there as the principle witness against his own mother.' This was the essential evidence that would prove administration of the poison, and which her son said was soda, which she often put in the beer. Jones told the jury to 'take the evidence as it was, and it stated the contents of the paper to be soda; after she had used part of it she put it back again into the drawer, not destroying it to conceal her guilt.' It was not poison, Jones said.

Finally, having separated every last fibre of the case, Jones said that although it was clear that William Constable had died of arsenic poisoning, 'he was not in a condition to say that the arsenic was taken by accident or by the man himself, but he was in a condition to say that it was not given by the woman.'

The judge summed up, and the jury deliberated for twenty minutes. From the five options open to them, they came back with a verdict of guilty, with a recommendation to mercy.

Mary was asked why sentence of death should not be passed. She exclaimed, 'I did not do it; I am innocent.'

Pollock, dismissing the jury's plea of mercy, put on the black cap and sentenced the prisoner to death.

He said, 'Anyone who reads or hears the short history of what has occurred today in this court, must feel that you insured the life of the deceased without his participation – that you claimed the money on the very day that he died – that you misrepresented his age and complaint, and almost his name, in entering him by a name by which he was not generally recognised. You appear to have been actuated merely by this sordid love of a small, an exceedingly small, sum, and for this you have destroyed the life of a near relative, and periled your own soul.'

Pollock was 'deeply affected' while passing sentence, and, a vestige of the eighteenth-century Cult of Sensibility, 'many of the ladies by whom he was surrounded were bathed in tears.'

The trial had lasted nine hours, during which time Mary had shown no feeling. 'It was only after sentence had been passed that she appeared at all conscious of the awful situation in which she was placed. Upon being removed from the dock she again protested her innocence.'

To the gallows

No one had been executed at Chelmsford for nine years. A petition to Sir George Grey, Secretary of State, to have Mary's sentence commuted, was got up almost as soon as the trial was over by the Society of Friends, or Quakers, in Chelmsford. They regarded her execution 'with horror' and wished to point out 'the manifest inefficiency of capital punishment in repressing crime, and the demoralizing effects of public executions in general, in attracting together large crowds of people, to witness such a revolting spectacle, and by this means to diminish in the public mind a sense of the sacredness of human life'. It was, they pointed out, over forty years since a woman was last executed in the town.

That had been Elizabeth Larghan, a soldier's wife living in Colchester, who had killed her baby at its birth to hide it from her husband. He was a private in the 18th Light Dragoons who 'had often upbraided her with his being reproached by his comrades, that she was with child before he married her' and that it was not his baby. She was executed in 1804.

The petition was eventually signed by 1,385 people; objections to capital punishment extended beyond the Society of Friends. It was presented to the Home Secretary by prominent local Quakers, including Sir Edward North Buxton, Whig MP for Essex South. Buxton was the son-in-law of Samuel Gurney, an important Quaker philanthropist who agitated against capital punishment and worked with Elizabeth Fry to improve prison conditions.

Pollock was asked to send his notes to Horatio Waddington, Grey's assistant. With incongruous gentlemanly bonhomie, his hastily scrawled covering letter was addressed to 'My dear Waddington' – they may well have been used to drinking brandy together in the same gentleman's club. 'I abstain from expressing any opinion of my own as you do not call for it,' Pollock wrote. His own speech on sentencing Mary was surely enough to show he was convinced of her guilt.

The deputation met with disappointment: Grey said that 'it was one of the worst cases that had come before him' and that 'proof of guilt was so evident' that he had to allow the law to take its course. He did comment, though, that the petition was 'a very important document, expressing, as it did, the decided opinion of so many persons in one town against capital punishment'.

On 5 August, Durrant, Mary's solicitor, wrote a letter to Grey. He pointed out that the jury had given the recommendation to mercy, 'which implies some doubt in their minds as to her guilt' and 'amounts to an expression of a wish on the part of the jury who tried her that her life should be spared.' He said that 'her frank admission at the coroner's inquest' of having bought rat poison and used it in the house, when no one could prove it, demonstrated her innocence. Then there was the evidence given by her son, 'which I have no doubt tended more than anything else in the minds of the jury to fix her with the crime.' Its inclusion was to show how poison was administered, except that her son had said it was soda, and that it was white, not the dark grey colour of Butler's Rat Poison. Durrant commented on the evidence given by Inspector Raison, which the newspaper did not print, but the solicitor asked whether 'independently of this man's statements, there was apparently sufficient to convict the prisoner.' Raison himself came off badly

– on 24 July, he had been dismissed from the Essex Constabulary, perhaps because of bad press; he was reinstated a week later.

Durrant's long letter was answered three days later in just one paragraph. Grey could find 'no sufficient ground to justify him, consistently with his sense of public duty, in recommending the prisoner to the clemency of the Crown; and to acquaint you that the law will, therefore, take its course.'

It isn't clear if Mary, sat in her cell in the old gaol in Chelmsford, was aware of the attempts being made outside its walls to save her. Her refusal to confess might indicate her innocence, but could be proof that she did know about the petition, and thought that by maintaining her innocence she would win her reprieve. Reporters were not allowed inside the prison, so what the newspapers were able to print about her last days came from the mouths of prison staff.

Her initial sulkiness gave way 'and she eats and drinks heartily, but still continues to assert her innocence, protesting that she has done nothing for which she ought to suffer.' This did not recommend her to the sympathy of the public, who wanted their condemned criminals to confess their guilt and leave this mortal plane with a clean conscience. But Mary would not confess – to those who believed in her guilt, this was stubbornness and a mark of her profligate character. But, if she wasn't guilty, her refusal to confess merely showed that they were about to hang an innocent person.

The prison chaplain and a Chelmsford curate tried to get her to confess but 'she manifested little sense of the awfulness of her situation, beyond a vague feeling of dread at being deprived of life, without any sign of repentance for sins, or desire to be forgiven them.'

On Saturday, 12 August, Mary was moved from the old gaol to the county gaol in Springfield. It had been built in 1830, and it is still in operation today, as HM Prison Chelmsford. Being moved to the prison where she would be hanged forced upon Mary her desperate position. She had to be supported to and from the van and 'on entering the woman's ward of the prison she uttered a piercing shriek, which was followed by a fainting fit' on reaching her cell.

She slept badly, 'frequently disturbed and restless, muttering imprecations against the witnesses who had given evidence, and who she said had sworn falsely.' The thought of James Simpson, her lodger, particularly riled her.

She 'declared with an oath, that if she could get at him, she would tear out his heart.'

On Sunday afternoon, her husband came to visit. She was glad to see him, but her conversation was 'extremely flippant, telling him she would haunt him if he married again, and giving trivial directions about the disposal of her clothes.' One gown in particular, which she claimed had cost her 13s 6d, she wanted to give to her sister, 'and the others were to be laid up till the little girl was old enough to wear them.' She possibly meant Robert's sister; the little girl was her 3-year-old daughter, Jemima. Clothing was expensive, and was often bequeathed in wills, so Mary's dividing up of her wardrobe is not unusual, although it seems out of place in the pathetic setting of a condemned cell. She wanted her children to wear mourning, and her husband a crepe band on his hat for two years; the tone of the newspapers reporting this seems rather snooty – as well as displaying ideas above her station, who, they might have said, would mourn a murderer?

She advised her husband to have nothing to do with the people who helped to convict her, 'he was not even, she said, to have any woman in the house for fear of her stealing things, but his sister was to make his bed.' Perhaps she thought Robert already had his eye on her replacement.

She told her husband that her spirit would watch over the children, and then said, 'Bob, tomorrow I shall meet your two children in heaven.' This might be their baby, William, who had been born just the year before, and perhaps another child who was stillborn and therefore was not recorded. She added, 'I have another husband to meet.'

On mentioning her first husband, 'she sank on the bed and shook violently.' The papers suggested this reinforced the idea that she murdered her first husband, but surely it would not be odd to exhibit a strong emotional response to the thought of being executed and meeting her first husband again, even if she hadn't killed him.

Robert and Mary spent an hour together. He had not brought the children to visit as 'the ladies at Wix advised him not, and he thought it best, on account of the expense, for he should not know how to get them home again.'

On his leaving, Mary said, 'Be sure and keep your promise – if you do I will not trouble you.'

Robert commented to the prison governor, 'She has been a very good wife to me.'

She thanked the kindness of the matron and the prison officer, she acknowledged the prison chaplain and the curate – but still she would not confess. During the evening, she spoke to the matron about her first husband and his death, saying 'that he was very sickly, and asked her for a basin of milk, and she gave him one, but he did not require another, as he was dead in three hours.' The press gleefully implied that she had poisoned the milk.

She slept badly once more, even though she had said 'she should not have died happy if her husband had not come to see her, but now he had done so she felt more comfortable.'

For the first time in nine years, the scaffold was erected over the prison gates. William Calcraft, who in his long career is thought to have hanged more than 400 people, was the executioner. It was somewhat of a homecoming for him – he was born in Little Baddow, just outside Chelmsford. Even as the sun was rising, the crowd began to gather. 'As it was nine years since an execution took place, it was expected that the assembly would be immense, and there were parties present from distant parts of the county, including several from Wix.' It was estimated that about 3,000 people gathered to see the spectacle of a public strangulation, and most of the crowd consisted of women.

The behaviour of the crowd at public executions had long been a contentious issue, part of the argument for abolishing capital punishment entirely. A carnival atmosphere filled the streets around the prison, 'that levity which is too often indulged in at these awful scenes.' Durrant, Mary's solicitor, reported to a meeting concerning the abolition of capital punishment some months later that, on the day of Mary's execution, 'a public house near the scene there was for the whole day a ribald assembly of young men and women, who were discussing the topic in the most revolting manner: there was no less than £20 worth of beer sold that day.' Opponents of capital punishment handed out leaflets 'and a prayer meeting was held about the same time at the independent chapel.'

Just after nine o'clock, the bell began to toll and Mary was led to a small room beside the scaffold. Once again, the prison chaplain tried to get her to confess: she would not. She climbed the ladder to the scaffold, unable to stand by herself, and moaned, 'Save me – save me' and 'Where is my dear husband?'

Calcraft fixed the noose around her neck, and placed a cap over her head. She turned to one of the prison officers who was holding her up, saying, 'Goodbye. May the Lord have mercy on my soul.'

The drop fell, and after three minutes of struggle as the rope crushed her windpipe, Mary May ceased to be.

Sometimes, a hanging could take up to twenty minutes. The *Chelmsford Chronicle* remarked that, 'being a stout heavy woman she appeared to die with a slight struggle.' *The Times* called her a 'portly woman' and the *Essex Standard* said that she was 'a stout lusty woman': her weight, described in undignified terms, meant her suffering was brief. It was part of the sentence that executed murderers were not given proper funerals, nor were they buried in consecrated ground, but were buried within the prison walls. It is a sad irony that Mary, who had entered her half-brother in a club whose sole purpose was to make decent funerals affordable, would not receive one herself.

A broadside ballad was written about Mary May and survives to this day as it was included by Henry Mayhew in his vast study *London Labour and the London Poor*. There were distinct types of ballads or broadsides issued as a trial approached – one might address the discovery of the crime based on inquest reports in newspapers, another would be about the trial, and still another would be a lamentation as the prisoner awaited their execution. Following the execution, another ballad would be printed as a confession. Ballads were sold in towns as well as the countryside and at executions, and were a way for people who had limited access to newspapers to find out about current events – albeit highly embellished versions forced through the balladeer's pen. Buying a broadside or song describing the prisoner's execution and its aftermath, while the prisoner was still alive standing on the gallows in front of the audience, seems not to have deterred customers.

The lamentation ballad had come into being in the late 1830s – before 1836, sentence of death usually had to be carried out within forty-eight hours. As one ballad seller interviewed by Mayhew put it, 'There wasn't no time for a Lamentation; sentence o' Friday, and scragging o' Monday.' Ballads were cheap and popular with ordinary people, and the words fitted

The Long Song Seller, from Mayhew's *London Labour and the London Poor*. He sold popular ditties, and songs covering current events.

popular tunes, albeit awkwardly. Sometimes they would be written to fit hymn tunes; Mary's can be sung to *All People That on Earth Do Dwell*. A description of the execution was followed by lyrics written in the first person, giving the impression of a gallows confession, even though Mary May did not make one:

The solemn bell for me doth toll, and I am doomed to die …

Not long afterwards, in the vestry of Wix church, Reverend Wilkins primed his pen and added another note in the burial register. Beside the entry for William Constable, he wrote: 'He was poisoned by his sister-in-law Mary May and she was hanged for it.'

In other houses

After the execution, the *Chelmsford Chronicle* decided to print 'various particulars relating to the previous life and conduct' of Mary May, which they had apparently had for some time in their possession. They claimed that 'it is well known in the village that she had led a most abandoned life' and that this was proved by her telling 'a gentleman of the parish that the boy who gave evidence against her, and who was born during her former husband's life, was the son of her present husband.' The identity of this gentleman is unclear, but it could well be Reverend Wilkins, who, as mentioned before, later wrote to the *Essex Standard* to tell them that Mary and Robert May had cohabited before their marriage. This could have been misreported as a query over William Everett's paternity. Continuing to frame her as an utterly immoral woman, the *Chelmsford Chronicle* also claimed that she had made 'indecent overtures to the policeman who had her in his charge'.

Once again, they brought up the issue of her late husband and her other children: 'She had long been suspected, before the present murder was brought to light, of poisoning other persons.' Reverend Wilkins claimed that at the time of William Constable's death, he was the only person to suspect Mary, so it is quite likely that it was nothing but retrospective gossip. It was only once her brother was found to have died from arsenic that questions arose over the earlier deaths.

Panicked hysteria was taking hold, poisoners lurking everywhere. 'Sudden and mysterious deaths, it is stated, have also occurred in other houses where she was intimate, with which it is believed she was connected; but the grave has now closed over her and her crimes, and it is useless to pursue the awful enquiry further.'

Mary was dead: another woman was in their sights. Hannah Southgate, a friend of Mary's, had lost her husband to a swift illness and she had married again soon after.

Was another murderer about to be unmasked?

Chapter 3

Tossicated

Ten days after Mary May's execution, Thomas Ham was exhumed from the churchyard in Tendring. His sudden death, over a year before, in April 1847, had been diagnosed as a burst blood vessel by the surgeon. Thomas's widow, Hannah, had been a friend of Mary May's; she had married again only three months after Thomas's death. Whereas Mary May's alleged motive was burial club money, Hannah, it was supposed, had killed to free herself to marry again. Until 1857 in Britain, divorce was only possible by a private Act of Parliament so was beyond the means of ordinary people – for most, the only way to end a marriage was by death.

Tendring parish church. The village hall, which was once the National School, peeps over the churchyard wall on the right-hand side of the photograph.

Hannah was born in 1819 in Tendring, a village 3½ miles south of Wix. She was one of eight children of James Angier, a labourer, and his wife Sarah, a poulterer. Hannah was not, as some rashly assumed, Mary May's sister or first cousin, even though they shared the same maiden name. Angier is a far from unusual surname in the Tendring Hundred; even an outcrop of Great Bentley is called Aingers Green.

Hannah grew up to be an attractive woman with a quick temper and a loose tongue. In December 1839, heavily pregnant, she married Thomas Ham, from Wix. Whilst Hannah was the daughter of a labourer, Thomas's grandfather, John Ham, had owned several properties in and around Wix. Thomas's father had inherited some of this property when John died in 1825, but it wasn't enough for him to live on as a gentleman of independent means – he was a blacksmith, and so was Thomas. Hannah and Thomas's first child, named Hannah, was born a month after their wedding, but only lived for eight weeks. Another daughter, Emily Lavinia, was born in 1841. More children were born to Thomas and Hannah, but only Emily survived.

They lived together unhappily. Their neighbours overheard quarrels, usually prompted by Hannah returning drunk, late at night. In her cups, she would say that if her husband didn't die soon, she'd kill him, and Thomas's mother saw her hit him with the handle of her whip after they had both been drinking. Thomas was a journeyman blacksmith; he didn't have his own forge and had to travel about to work, and a kick he had received from a horse as a child led to health problems. His income was unreliable, and Hannah contributed to the household purse by working as a higgler and poulterer, buying produce from farms and travelling to towns and villages to sell it. It is quite possible that Mary May got her idea to go higgling herself from seeing her friend clatter through Wix in her cart.

At some point in the 1840s, the Hams moved to Tendring. It could have been prompted by the death of Hannah's mother in 1844; her father had died by 1841, so Hannah's youngest sister was an orphan at the age of twelve. The Hams lived chaotically: like many people, they had a rodent problem and kept arsenic in the house. Hannah's was in the pantry, wrapped in paper, and she spread it on bread and butter, as did Mary May, to kill rats and mice.

Whether Hannah knew John Southgate of Bockings Farm before her move back to Tendring, or if she got to know him on her travels in her cart is unknown. However, at some point before her husband's death, Hannah was seen by several people around his house in Wix late at night and early in the morning. The son of a schoolmaster, John had become a farmer and property owner, and so was higher up the social scale than Thomas Ham. Ironically, it was John's father who was a witness to the will of Thomas Ham's grandfather; the other was Nathaniel Sorrell, a relative of this author.

The Hams quarrelled over Hannah's visits to John Southgate. Having stayed away for some time – the Hams' servant, Phoebe Read, stated that Hannah stayed away up to a fortnight at a time, but one wonders who looked after Emily in her absence – Thomas questioned her, and Hannah replied, 'I called to see my Johnny, and had a cup of tea with him.'

On another occasion, Phoebe heard Hannah say that she would marry John as soon as possible after her husband's death, the next day if she could.

Thomas replied, 'I don't think you will have the chance.'

Hannah said, 'Oh, I am sure to have him.'

'You must stop, madam, and get rid of me first.'

Hannah retorted, 'I can have him, and will have him; and so if you don't die soon I'll kill you.'

The Hospital Arms pub, Colchester.

Thomas Ham's last illness

Thomas last had work as a blacksmith in February 1847; lack of income added to the tension in the house. His mother would later say that Hannah had said 'she wished she could get rid of him, for he had no work to do, and she did not wish him to go to market with her, and that he was more trouble than he was worth.'

Daniel Levett Manthorpe, a surgeon from Thorpe-le-Soken, first attended Thomas for 'a painful affection of the stomach' on 29 March 1847. He didn't consider it to be dangerous, and he continued to see the patient occasionally, prescribing him a simple tonic.

Scraps of work came Thomas's way – in mid-April, he went to Bradfield with John Crampion, a pig-jobber. This intriguingly named job title denotes someone who deals in pigs, droving the animals, so it was physical work. Thomas told Crampion that he was unwell; chilly and cold.

On Saturday, 24 April, Thomas's health rallied, and he was about in the yard, cleaning out his stable. According to Phoebe, that day Hannah had gone to Harwich market. But Lucy Rowland, from Ramsey, remembered on that Saturday meeting Hannah in Colchester at The Hospital Arms pub on Crouch Street. They talked about an unfortunate widow called Mrs Wickham, whose brother-in-law had sold off her husband's belongings as soon as he had died. Lucy said Mrs Wickham should have sold her things before her husband's death – presumably her own belongings had been assumed by her brother-in-law too, as legally they were her husband's. Hannah told Lucy that her own husband was 'an afflicted man', and asked if anything happened to him, could his friends (meaning family too at this period) 'take her little property away?' Lucy explained that because Hannah had a child, they would not be able to.

Hannah said, 'That's all I want to know, and I be — if I don't give him a pill that he can't suck through a quill.'

Lucy asked how long Thomas had been ill, and Hannah said, 'Eight weeks, and for eleven weeks he had never earned her a penny.' She could not support him, and would not, 'for he was more trouble to her than a child.' She perhaps meant he had not had any blacksmith work, although pig-jobbing might not have earnt him much in his weak condition.

Hannah had not travelled 12 miles to Colchester just to gossip in a pub – the town seems to have been on her higgling rounds, as Lucy would later say that Hannah 'had been very kind in taking parcels to her son at the Hospital.' But was it a coincidence that she should ask Lucy about Mrs Wickham's property problems when her husband was to die only a couple of days later?

Thomas usually sat up waiting for his wife, but that night he decided not to, and went up to bed before Hannah came home. He had slept alone for some time – after Phoebe went into their service in the spring of 1846, Hannah had shared her bed. She said she wouldn't sleep in her husband's because she hated him – sharing beds with servants and lodgers was not unusual at the time. Like Hannah, Phoebe was caught in an unhappy marriage; her husband, a mariner called Henry Read, had abandoned her.

The next morning, Thomas didn't get up. Hannah gave Phoebe tea and toast to take up to him. Phoebe worked around the Ham's house, but also helped with the family business by plucking fowl with Hannah. Most of the evidence of what went on in the Ham household came from Phoebe, but each time she gave her testimony, remembering events that took place over a year earlier, it was confused and often contradicted what she had already said. Piecing together events from Phoebe's recollection becomes nearly impossible.

She initially said, at the inquest, that after the tea and toast, she had taken Thomas a glass of port wine, and that he had vomited half an hour after taking it – as arsenic can act quickly on the body, one might assume the arsenic had been in the port, but Phoebe had taken a sip and not noticed anything odd in its flavour. Later, however, she said that this had been on another occasion and that instead, on the Sunday when he fell gravely ill, he had drunk brandy. She remembered that Hannah made some gruel for Thomas, after he'd had the port. She recalled that Hannah had added powdered ginger, sugar and gin to the gruel and that Hannah had tasted it in front of Phoebe and said that it was good. But later, she said she wasn't sure if she had given the gruel to Thomas on the Sunday or at some other time.

Thomas vomited again and again, bringing up yellow and green fluid streaked with blood. He complained of terrible stomach pain and his throat was burning; he was thirsty but he struggled to swallow and several times he put a quill pen down his throat as if trying to dislodge something caught there. According to Phoebe, Hannah's less than sympathetic reaction was, 'Dear, I wish you wouldn't retch so; I know you do it on purpose to tease me.'

John Crampion, the pig-jobber, came to see him, and Thomas asked him to give him something that would help. John fetched him a wineglass of brandy, and asked Hannah for some hot water for it. He left it by Thomas's bedside. It was perhaps the memory of this brandy that had confused Phoebe.

His mother, Mary Ham, came to see him, and saw him retching but nothing came up. Because he had been unable to eat or drink, there was nothing left for his stomach to throw off. She offered to stay the night to sit up with him, but Hannah refused her offer. Asking that Hannah tell her if her son got worse, at nine o'clock Mary went home. She claimed this happened on the Sunday, which is the day Phoebe said Thomas fell ill, but Mary said Hannah's reason for not wanting her to stay was because 'she had no rest with him the previous night, and they should soon go to bed to get a night's rest' – which suggests he fell ill the day before. Either Hannah came up with a spurious reason for sending Mary away, or Mary's visit was on the Monday instead.

On Monday morning, Thomas asked Phoebe to fetch Manthorpe as 'he felt a great deal worse, and that he must have some remedy or he should die.' Hannah said, 'Dear, I am going to Thorpe, and I'll tell Mr Manthorpe to come.'

She asked him if she was to tell the doctor that Thomas felt better, but he replied, 'No, tell him I'm worse.'

Phoebe said Hannah left the house at three o'clock in the morning 'to go her rounds after fowls, as usual, and returned between twelve and one o'clock.' With her job requiring her to leave the house so early, we may find an innocent explanation for her being seen at five o'clock in the morning at John Southgate's house.

Once Hannah had returned, Thomas asked her if she had been to fetch Manthorpe.

'Yes, dear, and he told me he would come as soon as he could.'

By four o'clock, Manthorpe still had not arrived. Hannah said, 'Dear, I don't think there is any cause to send for him just now,' but Thomas insisted he felt very bad, and sent Phoebe to fetch the surgeon.

She found Manthorpe at home, and told him he must come at once, as Thomas was so ill that he was bringing up blood. Phoebe later claimed that Manthorpe was surprised.

'Dear me,' he said, 'Mrs Ham this morning told me he was better.'

But at the inquest, Manthorpe said he did not recall Hannah sending for him that day. If we believe Phoebe's testimony, this puts Hannah in a bad light – either she knew Thomas was very ill and told the surgeon he wasn't, or said she'd fetch the surgeon but deliberately didn't. If, however, we assume that Hannah was innocent, the fact that Manthorpe had been regularly visiting Thomas suggests she was blasé about the surgeon coming to see him again.

Manthorpe visited that evening. He told the inquest that he 'found him in a state of great exhaustion; he complained of great difficulty in swallowing, and of his throat.' He did not recall Thomas complaining of vomiting, but 'I considered him in a hopeless state, and did not, I believe, prescribe for him; I supposed he had ruptured a blood vessel.'

Hannah's sister Sarah Gardner and her husband Henry came to see Thomas, and at his request they stayed all of that night by his side. Henry was the butcher who, a few months before, had called on Inspector Raison's

	REGISTRATION DISTRICT					TENDRING		
1847	DEATH in the Sub-district of	Thorpe				in the	County of Essex	
Columns:–	1	2	3	4	5	6	7	8
No.	When and where died	Name and surname	Sex	Age	Occupation	Cause of death	Signature, description and residence of informant	When registered
186	Twenty seventh of April 1847 at Tendring	Thomas Ham	Male	29 years	Blacksmith	Rupture of Blood Vessel not certified	The mark of Sarah Gardiner Present at Death Tendring	Twenty ninth of April 1847

Death certificate of Thomas Ham.

help when someone robbed some meat from his cart. He is also another person connected with Hannah Southgate's case who is a relative of this author. Sarah saw Hannah try to give Thomas medicaments that she kept in a drawer, but he wouldn't take anything, and continued to cough up blood. In the early hours of the morning, Sarah said to Thomas, 'Wouldn't you like to die, and can't you see an interest in Jesus Christ?'

'No,' he replied. The vicar was not sent for.

At five o'clock on the morning of Tuesday, 27 April, Thomas called Phoebe to him and asked her to fetch a doctor. She sent Henry off in his cart, it being quicker by far than for Phoebe to travel by foot, and she waited in the Gardners' house for his return. By the time Phoebe got back, she found Hannah crying.

'Well, Phoebe,' she said, 'you won't have to go to the doctor's any more, for your master is dead. You hadn't left the house more than a few minutes when he died; I didn't think his death was so near.'

As Sarah was heading to Thorpe-le-Soken, the location of their district registrar, Hannah asked her to register Thomas's death. When Sarah asked what the cause of death was, Hannah repeated Manthorpe's diagnosis – a ruptured blood vessel.

It seems that Sarah stayed with her sister until Thomas's funeral, with Phoebe at the Gardners' house, looking after Henry and Sarah's six children. But Phoebe visited while Thomas's mortal remains awaited burial, lying in the bed in which he had died. She reported later that Hannah asked if she missed her master. Phoebe said she did, and Hannah responded, 'Yes, and it's a good miss too.' Phoebe claimed that Hannah then said she was glad Thomas was dead, and that if he hadn't died she would've killed him, adding, 'I shall have my Johnny, for I like his little finger better than the other's body.'

About three days after Thomas's death, Hannah told Phoebe, 'I shall be glad when your master's buried for I can't go upstairs, I feel so bad.'

As if frightened of the corpse, she asked Phoebe if she would go upstairs with her to look at it. Phoebe did so, and she saw Hannah take his head and pull it to one side, saying, 'Blast you, you're dead now, and I wish you had been dead years ago, and then I should I have had my Johnny.'

There were various superstitions attached to death at this time. Mirrors were covered in sickrooms to prevent the soul being trapped inside it on death – while he was ill, Thomas asked Phoebe to bring him the mirror so that he could look at himself. In Emily Brontë's novel *Wuthering Heights*, which would be published a few months after Thomas's death, the mirror in Cathy's sickroom is covered over when she thinks that her own face looking back at her is a ghost. A tradition that existed all over England, and was still practised in Essex at least as late as 1901, was 'telling the bees': 'If a death occurs in a house, even in the middle of the night, the first duty is to go into the garden and tell the bees; otherwise another death will take place within the year.' The hives were even dressed with black crepe. Perhaps Hannah was superstitious enough to have engaged in this too.

Thomas's body lay in the cottage for five days, unmourned and unmissed by his widow, until his burial in the churchyard of St Edmund's, Tendring on 2 May 1847. He was twenty-eight years old.

Throwing off her widow's weeds

Not long after Thomas's death (Phoebe said variously two or three days afterwards, or the day after his burial), Mary May came to dinner. Phoebe overheard Mary say, 'Well, it's a good job Tommy is dead.'

Hannah, standing over the frying pan, replied, 'Yes, it is, and if he hadn't died as he did I would have killed him. He was a nasty little blackguard, go where he will, and I never liked him.'

After the funeral – Phoebe claimed it was two or three days later, whereas John Peck, Wix's parish constable, said it was about three weeks later – Hannah decided to find 'her Johnny'. Following Thomas's death, John Southgate had gone down to London, and Hannah sent for John Peck to ask him where John was. For all that the locals were convinced of illicit intimacy existing between them, John had left the area without giving Hannah his address – either because he was suspicious of her husband's sudden death and didn't want to be implicated, or because they were not as close as people assumed.

Peck told her of a cabman at Shoreditch in East London who would be able to tell her. Hannah said she would go in a week's time, and asked Peck if she thought John would marry her if she could find him.

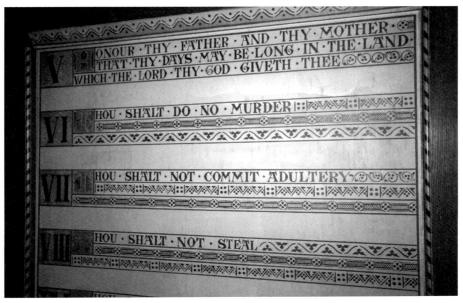

One of the panels displaying the Ten Commandments behind the altar in Tendring St Edmund's.

Peck replied, 'No doubt of it.'

Hannah did not stay overnight in London; she returned the same day and told Phoebe, 'I've seen my Johnny.'

With implausible surprise, Phoebe asked, 'What Johnny is that?'

'A young man from Wix, and he'll be here Sunday to dinner.'

Even though it was Phoebe who volunteered this conversation at the inquest, it is odd that she didn't know who Hannah meant by 'her Johnny', because on other occasions Phoebe had claimed to have heard Hannah tell Thomas, 'I like Johnny's little finger better than the whole of your body' – a phrase that, if those who gave evidence against her are to believed, she said with near-constant frequency.

In early June, Hannah arrived home one night tipsy.

'Phoebe, ain't you glad your master's dead?'

'No,' Phoebe said, 'I've no reason for it.'

'I am,' Hannah said, and, the image of sprightly glee, the widow took up her gown with both hands and danced up and down the house. 'Whoop,

Phoebe, I'm glad Tom is dead, for if he hadn't died as he did, I'd have killed him.'

The death of a spouse was not unusual in young couples at this time. In 1850, 19 per cent of marriages ended within ten years due to the death of a spouse, and 47 per cent ended within twenty-five years. Drunken joy exhibited by the surviving spouse was perhaps slightly less common. In the Victorian period, only 11 to 12 per cent of widows remarried. But it is no surprise that Hannah should have wanted to marry again: she was not yet thirty, and putting aside the affection she felt for John Southgate, as a farmer and property owner he offered her financial security.

On 28 July 1847, Hannah returned to St Edmund's church in Tendring, a bride once again. She married 'her Johnny' and the newly married couple went to live in Wix. In the churchyard, Thomas Ham slept in the silent darkness of his grave, deaf to the bells that rang in celebration; his coffin nursed a secret that in a year would be revealed.

'A passionate woman, one who talked recklessly'

And then, at the end of June 1848, the inquest was opened into William Constable's death. Lucy Rowland was riding with Hannah in her cart from Harwich, and asked her if she knew how Mary May was getting on. Hannah said she did not know in one way, but she wished she did in another. Lucy, perhaps hoping to pick up some interesting gossip about their local celebrity, asked Hannah if she knew much about her. She replied they had been like sisters together, but not lately, and she wished she had never seen her.

'Why?' Lucy asked.

'Because she's such a liar.'

Hannah tracked down Charlotte Elvish, who was giving evidence at the coroner's inquest. Charlotte was out gleaning in the fields, and she went down to the hedge with Hannah to talk. She asked Charlotte if she had told the inquest anything about her threatening to poison her husband.

'No,' Charlotte replied.

Hannah asked her if she intended to, and Charlotte said, 'I don't know; if anybody asks me anything I shan't tell any lies about it.'

Bribing Charlotte, Hannah asked her if she wanted anything.

'No,' Charlotte again replied. Hannah said she would give Charlotte anything she wanted if she went with her 'to make a liar and a fool of old Phoebe.'

Charlotte refused.

In the interval between Mary May's trial and execution, Lucy saw Hannah in her cart talking to Eliza Crisp outside Lucy's gate. On the Tuesday after Mary's trial, Eliza had asked Hannah if she knew how Mary had got on, the newspapers having not yet percolated down to Eliza.

Hannah told her that her acquaintance was condemned to be hanged, and said, 'I could not rest, and my husband went down and waited at Mrs Lowe's till two o'clock in the morning, and that was how I came to know it.'

Hannah went to market and on coming back asked Eliza if she'd heard anything else. Eliza said no, and Hannah asked what she knew of Mary, and if the condemned woman could keep a secret.

'Yes,' Eliza said, and as Hannah drove off, Lucy heard her say, 'Mary May has been a Briton up to this time.'

To those who had heard Hannah threaten to kill her husband and poison him, her questions about Mary May seemed highly suspicious. It may have

The Crown Inn, Tendring, now a private house.

been nothing more than Hannah's concern for her friend – very few people alive in Britain today can know how it feels to have a friend be condemned to death. But the other interpretation was all too obvious – that Hannah had poisoned her husband, and Mary May knew.

It was Inspector Raison once again who decided to investigate, either having been approached directly by these women or having heard rumours abroad. Hannah sent for Charlotte three times to go to her house, and asked her again if she would go with her to Mr Eagle's, where her former servant was now in service, 'to make a fool of Phoebe.' Charlotte refused to go, and just at that moment, John Southgate came into the kitchen with his brother and Police Constable Emson. Hannah winked at Charlotte and told her to hold her tongue.

On 22 August, John Peck was near the Southgate's house and told Hannah that he heard they were going 'to take Tommy up, as they suspected he was poisoned.'

Hannah retorted, 'They might take him up, for I used him as well as he used me, and before I would put up with what I have done, I would be hung.'

Her husband was with her and said, 'Hold your noise and no one can hurt you.' Her quick temper and careless threats had got her into enough trouble already.

Inquest

On 23 August, just over a week after Mary May was hanged, the inquest into Thomas Ham's death opened at the Crown Inn in Tendring, only a few houses along from the church. Now a private house, it had been a pub for hundreds of years. The road that runs north from Weeley to Tendring is called Crown Lane, and in front of the old pub is Tendring's village sign, which bears a crown. The name no doubt comes from the church's dedication to St Edmund, a ninth-century king of East Anglia and former patron saint of England, whose banner bore three crowns. At the time of the inquest, the landlord was Joseph Newcomb, yet another relative of this author.

The *Chelmsford Chronicle* briefly reported the inquest on 25 August, paraphrasing from a letter sent to them. They said the grounds were Mrs May's friendship with Hannah, and 'in fact their maiden names had been the same, and we conclude they were related.' Their correspondent had told them that Hannah was 'loose and irregular in her conduct' and claimed she had 'cohabited with a man named Southgate before her husband's death.' Ham was known to have money, he died suddenly with symptoms that looked like mineral poisoning, and Hannah married Southgate 'immediately' afterwards – circumstances that were enough to convince William Codd, Coroner, to open an inquest.

The inquest was over in three meetings. At the first, the only witnesses were Mary Symonds, who had laid Thomas out after his death and identified the exhumed body by the grave-clothes she had made, Phoebe and the surgeon. Phoebe talked about Thomas's symptoms and the progression of his illness, as well as the Hams' unhappy marriage and the threats Hannah made against her husband's life. Manthorpe testified as to Thomas's earlier complaint, and then what he witnessed on his sickbed visit just before his death. He went through the findings of his post-mortem – Thomas's viscera were not as decomposed as he had expected, which might show the presence of arsenic. But he could not prove this himself, so his son, Maurice, who was also a surgeon and had assisted at the post-mortem, took the bottled remains down to Professor Taylor in London.

Taylor performed his analysis on Friday, 25 August. It cannot have been pleasant working with viscera from a corpse that had been buried for over a year; he described the stomach contents being 'in a partial state of decomposition', giving out 'a quantity of ammoniacal vapour'. He found partially digested meat with 'a gritty feel, as if mixed with sand'. He tested this and found that most of the powder was white arsenic, and the gritty substance was sand and glass. He looked under the microscope and found the fibres of the meat 'were completely penetrated by the particles of arsenic' – had Thomas eaten arsenic-laced meat? Arsenic was also present in the liquid contents of the stomach, the coats of the stomach and in the middle of the small intestines. There were red patches showing that Thomas's stomach and intestines had been inflamed during life, so Thomas had ingested the poison before he died.

He sent his report to William Codd and on Sunday, 27 August, Hannah Southgate was arrested and taken to Colchester Gaol. The town's castle, a Norman keep, had been used as a prison for hundreds of years, but

The National School, Tendring. From an old postcard.

conditions were so bad that in 1835 a new gaol had been built in the town on Ipswich Road.

The inquest was resumed on Tuesday.

'It having become known in the neighbourhood that arsenic had been detected in the stomach of the deceased, the excitement prevailing in the neighbourhood had considerably increased, and long before the time fixed for holding the enquiry the Crown public-house, at which it was to take place, was surrounded by a crowd of persons, anxious to obtain a view of the accused.' Just as with the inquest into William Constable's death, so many people wanted to attend that the village school was requisitioned. It had been opened in 1842 and is now Tendring's village hall. A one-storey, redbrick building, with high-pointed gothic gables over the windows, and a zigzag pattern in dark grey bricks on the walls, it stands opposite the church.

Unlike Mary May, Hannah had a solicitor; John Henry Church was able to cross-examine the witnesses. This was a benefit that Hannah could enjoy as a farmer's wife, and was beyond the means of a labourer's wife like Mary: justice does not favour the impecunious.

Hannah, brought in by William Marson, governor of Colchester gaol, 'was very respectably attired, rather good-looking, and during the investigation frequently exchanged smiles with her husband.' Could the coroner, his jury, the inquest audience and newspaper readers accept that this attractive, well-dressed woman had behaved in a 'loose manner' and murdered her own husband?

The testimony varied; from the official, professional male voices of Manthorpe, Taylor and Peck, to the female tittle-tattle of village gossips. Church began what Hannah's defence counsel would continue at her trial – unearthing the long-held grudges and exposing the insubstantial innuendo of the women's accounts. There was more poison in their testimony than Taylor had discovered in Thomas's stomach.

When Mary Ham, Thomas's mother, told her story about Hannah hitting him with the handle of her whip, Church asked her if Thomas had been drinking – he had. Church found out, presumably from Hannah, the sad story of Thomas's only brother, John, who had committed suicide aged fourteen. The 1832 newspaper report said that John had an 'irritable temper' and after his sister had 'upbraided him for stammering, he told her he had a good mind to chop her head off with the bill hook he had in his hand.' He stormed off to the stables, and his sister spent an hour looking for him. She found him and, frightened, told her parents that 'her brother was standing up in the stable, with something round his neck.' Their father cut John down, but it was too late. While Hannah was thought to have poisoned her husband, Church set about trying to suggest that Thomas himself had ended his life. The idea that depression could run in families seems to have been current at this time. But his mother was dubious.

'He was frequently low spirited and melancholy, but I believe his wife to be the cause of it.' When she saw him on the Sunday before he died, 'his conversation seemed perfectly rational.'

Mary Ham reported that Hannah had said Thomas 'was a very bad corpse, and ought to be screwed down,' which implied Hannah had a reason for wanting a swift burial. Church extracted from her the fact that at the time of Thomas's death, she owed Hannah some money for butter and eggs 'and there had been a little ill feeling between us on that account.' Having shown that Mary was prejudiced against Hannah, Church tried the same approach with Phoebe.

Phoebe was asked about Hannah's children, and she responded that Hannah had 'told me that she had six children, all of whom were dead, except one, about seven years old.' She was asked if Mary May had looked after them – the implication seems clear, that with the press and local gossip having it that Mary had had sixteen children and murdered most of them, she had killed Hannah's children too, or had helped her to do so.

But Church intervened, forcing Phoebe to admit that she had had five children herself, and only one was still alive. Two had died in Stanway Union House, and, worst still for a nineteenth-century audience, the other two dead children were illegitimate, born after her husband abandoned her. Phoebe tried to turn this back, alleging that when she discussed the possible due date for the child she fell pregnant with before Thomas's death, Hannah had said, 'Phoebe, make haste and get rid of that cub.'

There was great sensation in the inquest room at this allegation, as Hannah, a woman they believed to be of loose morals, had apparently urged her servant to have an abortion.

Phoebe went on. She had said, 'No, I shall not do that.'

Hannah replied, 'Take, and knock it o' the head, and I will take you again.'

The newspaper reported 'increased sensation' at this – from an abortion, Hannah had apparently suggested child-murder.

Phoebe claimed Hannah had offered her 'something for me to do away with my child'. She told Phoebe 'she had bought a box of pills for me that would do it; and she put her hand into her pocket to take them out, but she said she had lost them, and I never saw them.'

This evidence has intriguing parallels with Lydia Taylor's allegations against Thomas Newport. It is entirely possible that a woman like Hannah, who may have been carrying on with another man while her husband was still alive, knew how to rid herself of an inconvenient pregnancy. But it may be that Phoebe was embroidering the truth, using threads from reports of the Clavering and Manuden cases. What better way to show how bad someone was in the nineteenth century, than to claim they encouraged abortions? When Church quizzed her further on it, she said she couldn't remember where the conversation had taken place, and there were no witnesses, which somewhat undermined her testimony.

Phoebe's child died when it was thirteen weeks old, and she returned for a little while to Hannah's service. At the time of the inquest, Phoebe was pregnant again – but not by her estranged husband.

Peck, the parish constable, gave his evidence about the Hams' unhappy marriage. He had overheard Hannah say she would 'go along with John Southgate' and he had seen her 'late at night and early in the morning around John's house'. Church asked Peck if Thomas drank, and if he had seen him 'in the company of abandoned females in Colchester'. Peck had not, and neither had he heard of such a rumour; Church was clutching at straws to paint Thomas in the same bad a light as Hannah.

John Crampion talked about Thomas's illness and even pointed to another motive for his murder: his friend had squirrelled away some money. He believed it was £30, whereas Phoebe alleged Thomas kept over £100 in gold under the bed. This motive was not quite as interesting as the illicit romance alleged between John and Hannah, but it does pose a question: was Thomas salting away Hannah's earnings that, before the law was changed by the Married Women's Property Act, legally belonged to him?

Professor Taylor had travelled from London to attend the second meeting of the inquest. His report was read out by Codd and printed in full detail by the *Essex Standard*. Taylor had written that 'nothing could have got into or out of the stomach since the death of the deceased.'

Church, clearly missing this point, or hoping everyone else had, asked, 'In a churchyard where there are several graves adjoining, is it not possible for the arsenic to pass from one body to another?'

All that this question managed to achieve was laughter from those gathered.

Taylor replied, 'I never met with such a case,' and the laughter carried on; inquests could be rowdy, even once they had moved out of the pub.

As Hannah was not on trial, and to stop the inquest going on at unnecessary length, Codd asked Church to restrict his questions 'in as narrow a compass as possible'. Church blatantly ignored him.

Charlotte Elvish gave evidence about the friendship between Mary May and Hannah Southgate, saying she'd often seen the two women together, and that Mary had said of Thomas, 'If he was my husband I would soon give him a pill.'

Charlotte claimed that Hannah replied, 'Yes, I'll be damned if I don't give him a dose one of these days; I'll learn him hait.' 'Hait' was a command used to make a horse turn left.

Charlotte reported that she told Hannah she was a fool to speak as she did, and that 'she had better take her horse and cart and go dealing, as she could by that means get as good a living as her husband could.'

Hannah's response was, according to Charlotte, 'Damn him, I am not going to leave him with my little money.'

The prisoner protested: Hannah shouted across the packed schoolroom, 'How false you are, for you know I never spoke to you for three years before Ham died.'

But Charlotte went on, reminding Hannah that she had called her to her house, begging her not to tell anyone that she had threatened to poison her husband; that when John Southgate arrived with his brother and PC Emson, she had winked at her. And then, when Charlotte came back from giving evidence at Mary May's trial, Hannah and her husband paid a visit to Charlotte at her house. Hannah had asked if Mary May had 'said anything at her trial'. Charlotte said no. Charlotte was implying that Hannah was asking if anything had been said about Thomas Ham's death, whereas Hannah could have meant, had Mary May confessed to killing William Constable? John had said, 'Let her be hung, as all such old brutes ought to be. It will serve her right.'

Charlotte had responded, 'John, you talk like a fool, and had better sing small, for it may not be all over yet.'

Hannah commented that she felt sorry for Mary; she didn't want her to hang. To Charlotte, she said, 'Ah, Charlotte, mate; he don't know all that I know.'

Charlotte replied, 'No; I don't suppose he does.'

The coroner objected to Charlotte's evidence, frustrated by the insubstantial tittle-tattle being aired in his court.

'Really, these observations must have some reference to something particular that came within your knowledge.'

Charlotte replied, 'I don't know what they meant in particular.'

She claimed to have no ill feeling towards Hannah, but she revealed she was renting a cottage from John Southgate, and was under notice to quit.

John piped up this time, saying, 'Why don't you pay your rent?'

'I can pay you,' Charlotte said, to John and everyone gathered, 'as it is only five shillings that I owe you.'

And then more bad blood between Charlotte and the Southgates was aired in the schoolroom: five years earlier, Charlotte had been charged with stealing potatoes from John. She claimed at the inquest that she had not been in custody for the theft, but her husband was. Mary May had been there as a witness, but 'we did not want her as the potatoes were not stolen at all.'

This is not entirely true: on 5 April 1843, Charlotte had appeared at the Essex Quarter Sessions, defended by Charles Wordsworth. At the time, she was living in a cottage that adjoined John's. He believed that his potatoes were being frequently stolen from his house, so he marked about twenty of them with a spot of ink, and clearly not bothered if his thief choked on them, stuck a pin into each potato. Not long afterwards, some of these potatoes were found in Charlotte's house, and John identified them as his property.

It could not be proven that Charlotte had stolen them – she had a lodger in her house at the time, and she did not get on with his wife, who may have stolen them to frame Charlotte. Wordsworth, in addressing the jury, took a slightly different angle, and said that under the law, 'a wife was presumed to be acting with the cognizance and under the influence of her husband' and he believed it to be so in this case. But an indictment against Charlotte's husband was ignored by the grand jury, and Charlotte was acquitted. Charlotte, in trying to prevent people thinking she had a motive for reporting Hannah's words, glossed over what had happened during her own brush with the law.

There may well have been another reason for Charlotte's eagerness to give evidence against Hannah Southgate: envy. Charlotte was a wheelwright's wife, so she had occupied the same social stratum as Hannah when she was married to a blacksmith. In a society that relied on horses, wheelwrights and blacksmiths were essential; whilst some scraped by, others could make enough money to live a comfortable middle-class lifestyle. Still others, just like some farmers, were able to amass enough money to buy property and end their days as gentlemen. On marrying John Southgate, Hannah had risen in the ranks.

Charlotte had been born in Fingringhoe in about 1811, one of nine children of Thomas Jaggard. He was a farmer, who had inherited a 55-acre farm in Fingringhoe from his father in 1812, but it was weighed down with a mortgage and annuities for Thomas's two young half-brothers. His father had married for a second time in 1807, just before he turned fifty, and Thomas was himself nearly thirty. This new wife, Charlotte (yet another relative of this author), may have inspired the name of Thomas's daughter. Although his brother continued to farm in Fingringhoe, Thomas Jaggard and his family moved across the river Colne to Wivenhoe and worked as a labourer; he had presumably run into financial difficulty and let out his farm. It was in Wivenhoe in 1837 that Charlotte had her first child, an illegitimate daughter. A year later, she married James Elvish. Thomas Jaggard's will, written in 1846, shows that his farm was still mortgaged, and he directed it to be sold, along with all his personal possessions, in order to pay off his debts; what little might be left was to be divided between his children.

Born a farmer's daughter but having slipped down the social scale, Charlotte may have felt that Hannah had got above herself.

For all that Church tried to mitigate the rumours circulating in the area about his client, there were some things that his cross-examination could not scotch. At the end of the second meeting, Inspector Raison, 'who has displayed much tact and zeal in the case,' passed on information to the coroner about other suspected poisonings in Tendring and in the nearby villages of Bradfield, Ramsey and Dovercourt. They all involved the deaths of husbands, and the *Chelmsford Chronicle* said it pointed to the existence of 'a most diabolical system' and that 'the disinterment of the bodies will no doubt be immediately ordered.' Was the zealous policeman about to deepen the witch-hunt?

After three meetings of the inquest, the jury had heard Taylor's evidence that arsenic had been found in large amounts inside Thomas Ham's body. They had also heard about Hannah's drinking, her quarrels with her first husband, her threats to kill him, and then her attempts to shush anyone who might give evidence against her. Along with that, there were suspicions hovering over other sudden deaths in the area. At eight o'clock in the evening of 4 September 1848, after several hours' deliberating, the jury returned their verdict of wilful murder against Hannah Southgate. The next day, she was conveyed to Springfield Gaol, to begin her long wait for the next assizes.

Hannah Southgate and the press

While the weekly Essex papers, the *Chelmsford Chronicle* and the *Essex Standard*, reported the inquest at length, other newspapers skated over the details and gave their readers what they wanted – scandal, death and moral outrage. The *Chelmsford Chronicle* erroneously claimed that Hannah Southgate and Mary May were sisters, but later rectified it. It's possible that it was Hannah's solicitor who made sure to correct the local papers, realising that whilst it wasn't good for Hannah that a friendship had existed between her and Mary May, the assumption that they were close relatives was even more injurious. The same had been printed in *The Times* and then copied by many newspapers across the country, but it appears they never corrected this; even today, the assumption is that they were family.

The Times's first piece on Hannah Southgate, on 29 August, followed Professor Taylor's discovery of arsenic in Thomas Ham's remains, and her ensuing arrest. Despite the inquest jury being nearly a week away from their verdict, their report was titled 'MURDERS BY POISONING' and began:

> Another most atrocious murder by secret poisoning has within the last two or three days been discovered in the neighbourhood of Wix, connected with which are some unpleasant statements, implicating one or more women with other murders, and which have led to the most painful excitement throughout this part of the country.

The Times took Mary May's friendship with Hannah to implicate her in the case, saying that Mary 'had urged and advised the commission of the dreadful crimes.' There is nothing in the far more in-depth reports we find in the local papers to suggest this at all, other than a conversation overheard by Phoebe between Hannah and Mary. In condensing the inquest, *The Times* ran with the Essex woman their readers were familiar with – Mary May.

Two days later they printed a longer report about the inquest, printing Phoebe's wobbly evidence at length. 'MORE POISONINGS BY ARSENIC' they declared, beginning their report with 'A horrible system of poisoning in this part of the county, termed the Tendring Hundred, was the subject of a lengthened investigation.' But at this point, only two poisonings had been confirmed in the Tendring Hundred – those of William Constable and Thomas Ham.

The following day, *The Times* printed a leading article on 'the case of the Essex poisoners'. The inquest into Thomas Ham's death had not been concluded at this point; there wasn't enough proven evidence for them to devote so much space to their article, which is why much of it reads as inflated rage, as insubstantial as the gossipy evidence produced against Hannah.

'Why should the practice of poisoning obtain rather in the marshes of Essex than elsewhere? In other counties as well as Essex wives are weary of their husbands' they wrote – but there were only suspicions of other husbands having been poisoned at this point, sudden deaths that people remembered, and with poisonings in the spotlight, found suspicious. Just as one swallow does not make a summer, one poisoning death does not make a poison-crime wave. However, 'Inspector Raison, who has been employed in the investigation of this as well as that of the Wix case, has made discoveries which prove that this is not an isolated crime. It is not a murder, but a result of a system.'

But what evidence did they present to prove there was a system? They could not print what Raison had discovered 'through a doubt of the manner in which the disclosures might operate'. Until a body had been exhumed and Professor Taylor had run his tests, there was no evidence to say that someone had been poisoned – there was only rumour. They admit this themselves, in saying that, after Mary's execution, 'the attention of the police was directed to the gossip of the countryside,' which led to Thomas's exhumation. All it seems to have required for a death to be included in 'the system' is for it to have been a sudden death of a man in an unhappy marriage, involving stomach pain and vomiting. Whilst this might indicate an intentional poisoning, it could equally – and perhaps more likely – indicate death from a violent stomach bug.

Even so, *The Times* continued to layer on the melodrama by reminding their readers of Madame Lafarge, whose case 'gave an impulse to similar crimes in France for a long period after its commission.' A leader written later in the same month, also about the Essex poisonings, claimed 'the existence of a state of things in real life more terrible than the horrors of the modern school of French novelists'.

Either intentionally or not, this played on the British fear of insurrection in the year of European revolutions. In February 1848, Louis Philippe, King of the French, abdicated and fled to England. The Chartists embraced the French revolutionary spirit and the audience in the cheap seats at Sadler's Wells theatre sang *La Marseillaise*. A middle-class meeting in Trafalgar Square, to discuss income tax, was overrun with Chartists, some yelling '*Vive la Republique!*' Threats were made that London would be sacked and burned, and in April *The Times* was warned that its offices were earmarked for destruction. By July 1848, the Prime Minister refused the Chartists' demands of votes for all men, saying the unrest in France had been caused by universal suffrage.

France represented the overthrow of societal norms; disorder caused by people violently wrenching themselves from their allotted stations in life, a threat to establishment and its control of power. Until the late eighteenth century in Britain, a woman who murdered her husband was convicted of petty treason and burnt at the stake; the family was the state in microcosm and the head of the household was monarch. The very idea that women were, en masse, colluding to murder their husbands, like Radicals conspiring to overthrow the establishment, fed into very potent anxieties current in Britain at the time. *The Times*'s report was reprinted in newspapers across the country, even in the *John O'Groat Journal*, published nearly 700 miles away from Tendring.

Even if Chartists and Radicals were not easily controlled, these murderous women who perverted the natural order of things could be routed. *The Times* believed that, while France had copycat poisoners following Lafarge, Britain would not, thanks to 'the certainty of detection, and the equal certainty that the culprit will pay life for life on the gallows a few weeks after the perpetration of the crime, without any drapery of sentimentalism, or interest excited in her fate'.

Of course, it was in vain to expect the execution should happen within weeks – whilst this was the case with Mary May, who, it must be recalled,

Ramsey parish church.

was executed for murdering her half-brother, not her husband, the other cases that were allegedly part of the 'poisoning system' were all deaths that had happened years before.

People mutht be amuthed

Following the outcome of the inquest, there would be a wait of six months until Hannah Southgate stood trial at the Easter Assize. In the meantime, as Mr Sleary said in Dickens's *Hard Times*, 'people mutht be amuthed.' Two men, whose names have since been lost to history, travelled to the Tendring Hundred, and claiming to be variously from the Home Office and from *The Times*, managed to wheedle various pieces of gossip-infused information from the locals. They were 'a couple of adventurers', who the *Essex Standard* said had hoped to get 'two-pence per line for their compilations – the more exaggerated the more saleable'.

Pretending to be residents of north-east Essex by signing their production 'Thorpe, Wednesday, Sept 13', their article was printed in *The Times* the following day. Its starting point seems to have been the recent articles in *The Times* about the Essex cases, but it is littered with errors and exaggeration. And, where the newspapers averred they would avoid printing anything about the forthcoming investigations, the 'adventurers' did not hold back and made the most of the information they had gathered on their trip to Essex.

There was, they claimed, every reason to fear 'that the husbands and children of a great number of women who were on habits of intimacy with Mrs May and Mrs Southgate have been destroyed.' It was the first article to mention there was to be an investigation into the suspicious death of Nathaniel Button, but they managed to get crucial details wrong. They said that he died in Ramsey on 30 September 1846, 'a few days after the death of Mrs May's husband'. Highly suspicious if true – but it wasn't. Nathaniel had died in 1844, and Mary May's first husband had died four years earlier. It was true that people had only become suspicious because his widow, Mary Elizabeth, had recently posted banns in church to marry again, but decided to postpone the marriage 'to see whether they would pull Button up.' This was hardly a hasty remarriage, and it would surely be difficult to allege his wife had killed him in order to be with another man when she had waited nearly four years after his death to marry again.

But most importantly, it was alleged that Button's wife had been a friend of Mary and Hannah, and the fervour surrounding the cases was such that a friendship with them made any widow automatically suspect.

They claimed Nathaniel had been 'seized with sudden illness after partaking of some food which had been prepared by his wife' and that he 'had frequently been heard to say he was afraid to take anything from his wife, as he was convinced she wanted to poison him.' In a parallel to the Ham/Southgate case, they claimed Mary Elizabeth had been 'criminally intimate with a man named "Bobby Peck"', and that 'almost immediately after the death of Button, Peck also died in a sudden and mysterious manner.'

This wasn't enough; they revealed yet another suspicious death, that of Palmer, 'who died shortly after Button under somewhat similar circumstances. Almost immediately after his death Mrs Palmer left Ramsey accompanied by a paramour with whom she had long been intimate.' Just like Nathaniel, he had died within a few hours of eating some food prepared by his wife.

This is Samuel Palmer, who was buried in Ramsey on 6 December 1844, two months after Nathaniel Button. Samuel's abode in the burial register is given as St Osyth, so his widow's sudden removal from Ramsey may indicate nothing more sinister than the prosaic fact that she went home.

Another husband who had allegedly been shoved off this mortal coil by his wife was 'a man named Brudger' from Great Holland, who had 'died some time since, suddenly and in great agony.' They may have fallen foul of the north-east Essex accent, or a typesetter who was unable to decipher their handwriting, as there was no one of that name in Great Holland at the time – they perhaps mean Bridges. Thomas Bridges was ten years older than his wife, Mary. She was his second wife, and when they married in 1837, she had been a widow. He died in June 1847, aged fifty-one. The article alleged that not only was the husband's death suspicious, but the deaths of their children were too, and they would all be exhumed.

And even Phoebe Read was implicated. Church's cross-examination, revealing that she had lost four children, brought her under suspicion. But in their scramble to paint as lurid a picture as possible of the Essex cases, they wrote that all five of Phoebe's children were illegitimate, which wasn't true, and that all of them would be exhumed. Considering that two of her children died in the workhouse, where Phoebe would not have had much access to them, it seems very unlikely that she would have been able to poison her children, even if she had wanted to.

The dead children of Thomas and Hannah Ham had 'in the language of the neighbours, "dropped off short" and were supposed to have been "white powdered".' These deaths, they assured their readers, agog for more horror, would be investigated as well.

They made the grand claim that 'most, if not all, owe their origin to the existence of what are, in this part of the country, called "death clubs",' which links the crimes back to William Constable's murder. They assured their readers that Hannah Southgate was a member of a club, as were 'the other persons whose names are implicated in these shocking affairs'. But no burial clubs were mentioned at all at the inquest into Thomas Ham's death, or the subsequent trial.

The article, including its mistakes, was reprinted all over the country – even in the pages of the local Essex newspapers, and eventually on the other side of the world once news had reached Australia and New Zealand. It seems that the article's writers submitted it to other papers, as well as it being copied, as was the norm. *The Observer* printed a slightly longer version, which included a description of the Tendring Hundred that made it sound like a bleak, godless place. The people 'reside chiefly in small farmhouses and cottages on the roadside, in most instances a long distance from the church or any place of worship.' Proper instruction was 'of the most indifferent kind'. They said 'Brudger' in Great Holland had eaten dumplings before his death, which has echoes of Catherine Foster's case tried in 1847. They claimed that it was 'a confession made by May previous to her execution' that sent the authorities on the scent, but as is clear from the reports at the time, Mary May went to her death having confessed nothing at all.

The Times followed this up with another leader, full of bombast and lacking much fact. They compared the events to French novels by Dumas and Sue, and then, completely ignoring the fact that it was the deaths of two grown men that had been caused by arsenic poisoning, they wrote instead about the murder of children in novelistic tones:

> As you pass through a country village in England, and see the children playing in the sunshine, can the mind admit the conviction that in many instances they are predoomed to a lingering and painful destruction; that the blooming cheek *must* soon grow pale, the rounded form be worn down by an emaciating fire from within, and the changing expression of childhood give way to the monotonous aspect of death, and that all this will be the work of their parents' hands?

It was once again an opportunity to bemoan the existence of burial clubs, and *The Times* adopted the voice of moral crusader: 'Nothing but a conviction that this infernal system has taken strong root in the country would induce us to bring such a subject forward.' They linked it explicitly with the cases that Chadwick had mentioned in Manchester – but whereas in the north of England, there had been cases involving the poisoning of children in burial clubs, in Essex at this point, it only involved the death of one adult man.

The Nelson's Head inn, Ramsey, now a private house.

The curious case of Nathaniel Button

Nathaniel Button was exhumed from Ramsey churchyard at noon on 20 September, and was taken in a cart down the hill to the Nelson's Head inn where the inquest was opened by William Codd. It emerged that he had been a member of the Maybush Friendly Society in Great Oakley, and so parallels were drawn at once in people's minds with the death of William Constable. *The Times* erroneously claimed that Mary May had made a private confession before her execution that 'afforded a clue to a system which, is it feared, is capable of most extensive proof, and will result in the conviction of a large number of women who have adopted the practice of poisoning their husbands and children for the purpose of obtaining the fees which are granted by what are in this part of the country termed "death clubs".' The club was to pay £8 on Nathaniel's death, but John Collings, the carpenter who identified Nathaniel's coffin when it was exhumed, said the widow was not paid the whole amount because 'we thought she would not defray the expenses of the funeral.' The verbal evidence made it plain that Nathaniel was generally a healthy man who had fallen ill very quickly, and whose wife was apparently indifferent to his sudden illness. But as usual, Codd could not proceed without a toxicological report.

To keep their readers entertained until the inquest was resumed, *The Times* recycled a piece they had written two years previously, their 'observations' on the poisoning cases in Norfolk and Essex. They clearly meant Sarah Chesham's cases, but did not name her, and once again incorrectly wrote that the events had taken place in Littlebury, 7 miles from Clavering. Had they forgotten Sarah had been acquitted? As before, they wrote that the woman 'was so well known to be a poisoner, and so generally suspect of even a gratuitous exercise of her art, that mothers used to keep their infants within doors when she was seen prowling about the village' and that she 'was at last detected by being observed to slip something into the mouth of a little child whom she accidentally met in the fields.' But it was no truer in 1848 than it had been in 1846, when this melodrama had first been scripted by *The Times*.

Playing on fears that another epidemic of cholera was about to arrive in Britain, they called the poisonings 'a moral epidemic far more formidable than any plague which we are likely to see imported from the East'. What it required, they decided, were restrictions on the sale of arsenic, and recalling Happisburgh, said that the coroner should 'not be circumscribed by the economy of his paymasters.' *The Times*, it was later claimed, did not blindly follow public opinion, but under the editorship of John Thadeus Delane at this period, 'was able to create it.' In the case of poisoners, they certainly did.

A few days later, *The Times* printed a terse letter from the vicar of Littlebury, requesting they correct the error they had made in claiming that the poisonings had occurred in his village. Ironically, the vicar's surname was Wix.

The second meeting of the inquest, in early October, was to be its last. Nathaniel's body had been so decomposed that the post-mortem could give no indication of poisoning, and Professor Taylor could find no arsenic at all in the viscera he analysed. In fact, the body had decomposed so much that Taylor could not find the stomach amongst the adipocerous mass that had once been human organs. He explained that if there had been arsenic in the body, it could have escaped due to the putrefaction of the organs, and water seeping into the coffin could have washed it away. Ammonia, produced by decomposition, could have dissolved any arsenic. Taylor looked to the physical symptoms suffered by Nathaniel and he believed they were not typical of arsenic poisoning. He urged the coroner to compel the jury to return a verdict of death by natural causes.

Taylor was not trying to downplay the investigation – his detailed report, printed in full by the local papers, included fiercely unpleasant descriptions of the decomposed organs, and he included a letter to William Codd explaining how hard the analysis had been:

> I cannot tell you the amount of mental and bodily labour this case has cost me. The chemical analysis occupied a week, and the details, had they been fully given, would have added many folios to the report. I have been almost poisoned with the effluvia, and for the last few days have suffered from a desperate headache. The case, in every point of view, required a most strict investigation.

Codd asked the jury to return a verdict as Taylor recommended, but the jury was not satisfied. They said they wanted to return an open verdict in case more evidence came to light, and after half an hour's deliberation, their verdict was that Nathaniel had died of retching and diarrhoea, but there was no evidence to show how.

Aware of the number of locals in the room, as well as the presence of newspaper reporters, Codd took the opportunity to make his own response to the wildly inaccurate 'two-penny-a-liner' article that had been circulating in the press. He said that it had been 'calculated to lead to much misapprehension, and to produce unnecessary excitement.' Whereas the article had claimed he had been passed a huge amount of evidence, he had, in fact, received no evidence at all. He had looked into three cases of suspected poisoning 'at Bradfield, St Osyth and another place, which he could not then immediately recollect', and having taken pains to consider them, decided there wasn't 'sufficient ground to warrant him in interfering in any one of them'.

Despite this, he did not entirely scotch the rumours that were circulating – he said he believed there really was a 'system' operating in north-east Essex and that children in the area 'may have been unfairly dealt with.' He said that if he did have sufficient grounds, he would not hold back from investigating, and that he wanted medical men who were called to deathbeds to 'pay more regard to the symptoms of parties they were called upon to attend than appeared to have been the case in several instances' he was involved in.

His fighting words might have been intended to deflect criticisms that police and coroners received from not investigating suspicious deaths. Pressure 'to keep down the county expenses', as one correspondent to *The Times* put it, was limiting the number of inquests that should have been held.

At the end of October, *The Times* published a leader calling for the restriction on the sale of poisons by chemists, written in its characteristically melodramatic style. The man seeking to destroy himself 'need but cross his threshold, and he will be invited to the shops where, for a few pence, he can purchase DEATH for himself or others.' The poor wretches' attention is attracted by the chemists' 'gaudy and transparent vases, red, green, and blue, illuminated from behind by jets of gas'. This different angle was impelled by the attempted suicide of Sarah Rich with an overdose of laudanum, but they still mentioned the Essex cases, claiming, 'had a difficulty existed in obtaining the arsenic with which the crimes were perpetrated, it is more than probable they would never have occurred.' They were corrected in this assumption by a chemist from Kelvedon in Essex, who said that arsenic was so widely used in farming that 'I very much question whether a chymist [*sic*] was ever applied to for the poison by the persons who used it.'

The 'epidemic from the east' was on its way. Would enterprising murderers conceal arsenic poisonings amongst the cholera deaths? In August, *The Times* commented that the government were making the country more vulnerable: 'The cholera has been steadily advancing, and the House of Commons has been just as steadily engaged in mutilating the Health of Towns Bill, our only safeguard against the ravages of this terrible calamity.' And in October, on the day *The Times* had melodramatically written of chemists selling DEATH, it reported that there were no cases of cholera in London, but 'the pestilence was spreading in Edinburgh.'

The trial of Hannah Southgate

Hannah had been in Springfield Gaol for several months by the time she stood trial in March 1849, but her incarceration had had no ill effect on her appearance – she was still an attractive woman. Her husband's wealth meant that she had presumably been kept comfortably in prison, and she was able to retain her own barrister, William Ballantine from the Old Bailey. In his memoirs, he described her as 'a young woman of somewhat prepossessing appearance' and the newspapers commented that she 'was very respectfully dressed.' The *Ipswich Journal* went further, almost like the caption from a fashion plate: 'The prisoner, whose deportment was very firm and collected, was well dressed. She had on a squirrel tippet, and wore a black veil, her hands being folded in a squirrel muff, appearing altogether in the attire of a respectable farmer's wife.'

This may have been quite intentional on Hannah's part, to make her alleged drunkenness and immoral behaviour seem unlikely, based on the role she had adopted and presented to the court. Dress was an important way marker for Victorians as they travelled through society, and the idea that appearance was an outward indication of inner morality tied in with the increased popularity in physiognomy and phrenology. You could, it was believed, tell someone's character from their face, from the bumps on their skull and height of their forehead, and the contents of their wardrobe. Oscar Wilde took this to an extreme in *The Picture of Dorian Grey* – no one suspects Dorian of his dark deeds as he always appears fresh and handsome, but the secret portrait shows how he should have looked as his evil ways destroyed and contorted his features.

The judge at the Easter Assize was Baron Parke. Just as at Mary May's trial, Ryland and Rodwell were prosecuting, and Ballantine was defending with Thomas Chambers, who had also defended May. It is possible that Church, Hannah's solicitor, had helped to select the barrister; his father was an attorney-at-law and the family were originally from London, so could well have known Ballantine personally as well as professionally. Ballantine had been called to the bar in 1834, but Hannah was one of his first clients who stood trial for their life.

Ballantine is an interesting character, involved in some of the most famous trials of the nineteenth century. In 1864, he successfully prosecuted

William Ballantine, from *Vanity Fair*, 1870, after the Mordaunt divorce trial.

Franz Müller for the first railway murder in Britain, and he defended the Titchbourne Claimant in 1871. He earned his portrait caricature in *Vanity Fair* magazine when in 1869 he refused to question the Prince of Wales at the Mordaunt divorce trial. Famous for his unrelenting cross-examinations, he would not cross-examine the Prince of Wales even though it meant he lost the case for his client, because it would have made a perjurer of the prince.

He was considered a buck, the Victorian gentleman who was at heart a Georgian, and despite his marriage in 1841, he continued to carouse in the West End with actors and authors. He was fond of the genial Dickens and his cheery laugh, and was a friend of Bulwer-Lytton, with whom he played while the novelist scribbled ideas on scraps of paper. He often met Thackeray but disliked him; 'He was egotistical, greedy of flattery, and sensitive of criticism to a ridiculous extent.' Ballantine provided the model for Anthony Trollope's barrister Chaffanbras in *Orley Farm*. He seems to have appreciated Bulwer-Lytton's fondness for crime in his novels, basing his plots on real cases. That said, he seems not to have noticed the link with *Lucretia* and Sarah Chesham, but was aware that it was partly inspired by the case of Wainewright. Unlike *The Times*, which was so mocking of Bulwer-Lytton's literary ability, Ballantine thought the prologue to *Lucretia* 'one of the most powerful pieces of writing that ever came from Lord Lytton's pen'.

He disliked forensic evidence in trials, wary that its use risked proceedings drifting 'into mere medical and scientific questions'. And well he might – ten years after defending Hannah, he faced Professor Taylor again when he was prosecution at the poison murder trial of Dr Thomas Smethurst. Having won a conviction, there was an outcry as 'a medical war was waged with great vigour in the newspapers' over issues with Taylor's analysis.

Ballantine was slightly above average height, but his 'lean, cadaverous appearance' perhaps made him appear taller. His voice had a drawling tone, 'half infirmity, half affectation', which contrasted with the booming, melodramatic style of other barristers. Despite this he had a reputation as a fearsome cross-examiner, perhaps his drawl lulling witnesses into a false sense of security.

Serjeant Jones had defended Sarah Chesham and Mary May by presenting them as 'good women', highlighting their kindness and attentiveness to those they had been accused of murdering, contrasting this with crimes so unspeakable, they could not possibly have committed them. Ballantine, however, took a different approach. In his closing speech, he called Hannah 'a passionate woman, one who talked recklessly' and said that Thomas Ham only consumed arsenic through Hannah's carelessness and poor housekeeping; the arsenic 'might have remained on the end of a knife, which had not been cleaned; and thus might have by sheer accident spread with the butter upon the toast.'

His cross-examination was not so much to prove Hannah's innocence as to undermine the character and therefore the trustworthiness of those who gave evidence against her. This may partly have been because he thought Hannah was guilty, whereas Church was 'vehement in expressing belief in his client's innocence.' Church wanted to call certain witnesses, but Ballantine, 'governed by my convictions, absolutely refused to do so, offering at the same time to return my brief.' It was refused, so Ballantine continued as Hannah's defence counsel, but without calling any witnesses for her. Church also wished to challenge one of the jurymen, but again, Ballantine refused, believing that 'using this privilege produces an unfavourable effect' – it would make Hannah look more guilty.

Phoebe Read, who was the main witness in the case, was not a particularly effective deponent, because she struggled to remember the events that happened two years earlier, perhaps floundering under the pressure of being in court. *The Times* remarked that she 'gave her evidence in a very unconnected and careless manner; and it was with considerable difficulty that a direct or clear answer could be obtained from her.'

But Ballantine undermined her evidence further. The conversation between Hannah and Mary May had, Phoebe admitted, only been partly overheard by her while Hannah fried some eggs. He made her tell the courtroom that her husband left her five years ago, and that she 'had three children since.' And why did she leave Hannah's service? Because Hannah had accused her of stealing a tea-kettle. And was this the only time Phoebe had taken things she shouldn't have? She admitted to having tasted some of the port that she took to Thomas Ham, and there was laughter in the courtroom. Did she do it for fear that Hannah had poisoned it? No, Phoebe said, 'I have often heard her say she would, but I never thought she meant it.'

Phoebe tried to defend her actions – the three illegitimate children born by three different men were Hannah's fault, she claimed, 'through Mrs Southgate filling the house with men.' And all three of those children were dead.

Surely it was no wonder someone in the Ham household had been killed by arsenic – according to Phoebe, the poison was kept 'screwed up in a piece of paper in the pantry; the poisoned pieces of bread were thrown away sometimes in the gutter, or where I could find a place; I may have thrown them sometimes in the swill tub; the butter used to be kept in the pantry.' Each semi-colon indicates where Phoebe was asked a question – Ballantine prodding answers from her to imply that Thomas Ham had ingested the arsenic by accident.

Asking Phoebe about her churchgoing habits, she replied, 'We never went to church or chapel, neither I nor my mistress.' Whereas Sarah Chesham had benefited from a vicar who believed in her, and Mary May suffered from the energetic interference of a vicar who didn't, Hannah had no vicar at all.

Phoebe was not the only witness to endure Ballantine's intrusive questioning. After Charlotte Elvish had given her evidence, claiming that Hannah had approached her to 'make a liar and a fool of old Phoebe,' Ballantine winkled out of her the fact that Phoebe was 'no great friend of mine' and that her sister, Mary Ann King, had fallen out with Hannah. He brought up the issue of the stolen potatoes and Charlotte admitted that John Southgate's father had evicted her, but she claimed not to be angry with him, even though Hannah had said she could remain in the cottage if she asked John. 'I said I would rather live in the street than go and ask him.'

Jane Harvey, a neighbour of the Hams, attested to their unhappy marriage. While the prosecution got her to claim that Hannah had said that if Thomas did not die soon, she would kill him, Ballantine made Jane admit that Hannah had been in her cups when she made her threats. 'They used to quarrel when she came home late at night "tossicated",' she said. The *Essex Standard* printed Jane's mispronunciation just as she had said it.

The most gossipy evidence of all came from Lucy Rowland and Eliza Crisp. Pouncing on the fact that Lucy had her conversation with Hannah in The Hospital Arms pub, Ballantine made her tell the court she had been drinking half a pint of porter at the time, and that she had not been examined before the coroner, thus undermining her evidence. It was under Ballantine's cross-examination that Lucy admitted Hannah had often taken parcels to her son while in hospital in Colchester, so he was able to paint a more favourable image of his client.

Ballantine had researched the other poison inquests in the area – easy to do with the reports appearing in *The Times*. He realised Eliza Crisp had given evidence at the Nathaniel Button inquest, of 'threats made by the wife against the husband. It turned out in that case that the husband had never been poisoned at all.' She said she had known Mary May very well. Perhaps Ballantine asked her about any acquaintance with Mary to demonstrate that many people were her friend, without it indicating criminality.

The medical evidence was of great importance. Manthorpe senior described Thomas's symptoms and what he found at the post-mortem, and his son proved that he had taken the jars containing Thomas's viscera to Professor Taylor.

Taylor went through how, in layman's terms, he performed the analysis, and what it meant: Thomas Ham had died from being poisoned with arsenic, and it was likely to have been taken on the Sunday morning. He had examined one-third of the stomach and found about five grains (320mg), which would amount to about fifteen (1g) in the whole body – two or three grains (130–200mg) were sufficient to kill.

Only one question was asked in Taylor's cross-examination by Ballantine: was he sure he had found sand? He was. Rodwell, prosecuting, re-examined him on this point, and Taylor said, 'The sand might have been in the arsenic, to adulterate it.' Clearly, if someone had meant to kill someone with poison, adding sand, and as Taylor also found, ground-up glass, would add to the internal damage caused, but it was apparently common for arsenic to be sold in that condition when used for killing rats. It doesn't seem to have been addressed at the trial or at the inquest where Hannah had bought the poison, but so many people testified that she was known to have arsenic about the house, it wasn't necessary. And with her horse and cart, she could have travelled wherever she wished in order to buy it.

It was time for Ballantine's speech, which he made at some length. He argued that the evidence was too inconclusive to support so serious a charge. He blamed rumours that had spread about the county: 'He knew not how that female gossip and chattering, of which they had heard so much, might have magnified matters till they presented themselves as matters of importance.' Having made certain assertions to their neighbours, they could not withdraw what they had said. He felt that Ryland, in his opening speech, had made observations that 'conveyed impressions not at all warranted by the testimony adduced, and yet calculated to prejudice the minds of the jury against the prisoner.' Mary May, he said, was nothing to do with this case and should not have been mentioned, and that little stock should be put by the words of Phoebe Read. Phoebe 'had lost children by death; and would be as much disadvantaged by her intimacy with May, as the prisoner at the bar could be.' Phoebe's evidence had been full of contradictions and improbability, and as was only too clear to the sensibilities of the time, she had a bad character.

He believed it was not proved that 'criminal intercourse' had occurred between Hannah and John Southgate, which – ignoring the gold under Thomas's bed – removed the alleged motive for murdering Thomas Ham. 'On the contrary she had busied herself in gaining an honest livelihood in a respectable manner' – the hard-working Hannah was merely a victim of her own reckless tongue. He explained away the arsenic, which he incorrectly claimed had been a small quantity, as an accident caused by bad household management.

Although it entailed a long stay in prison, it was perhaps as well for Hannah that so many months had passed since the Essex poisonings were mentioned in the press. Still, Ballantine addressed the fact that the case 'had excited great attention, not only in this county, but among the public at large' and that the jury should 'be governed by the evidence alone', and to put aside whatever opinion they had formed on the matter before they were called to be jurymen. Claiming there was so much doubt in the case, he called for an acquittal.

At about half-past six, as the judge began to sum up, the reporter for the *Ipswich Journal* dashed from the courtroom to make the 40-mile train journey back to Suffolk. In their report of the trial the next day, they made great fanfare of having received the verdict via that wondrous invention, the 'electric telegraph'.

It took two hours for Parke to go through the evidence, 'not unfavourably to the prisoner', Ballantine thought.

While the jury deliberated, Parke, who was sitting near Professor Taylor, commented to him that he was surprised that so little arsenic had been found.

Taylor replied that if he'd been asked the question, he would have to say that what he found proved in fact that a very large amount had been taken. This was the fault of the prosecution, who had not asked the question, and because Parke had found this out by accident, he could not use the information. Ballantine, who had asked Taylor just one question, congratulated himself on his 'first lesson in the art of "silent cross-examination"'.

Having sat in the jury box for the best part of twelve hours, it only took the jury a few minutes to reach their decision: not guilty. The juror whom Church had objected to was one who believed most strongly in her innocence. Hannah, in her respectable squirrel fur outfit, could finally go home to 'her Johnny'.

Murder in Sussex

A few months after Hannah was acquitted, another woman was in the dock for poisoning: wretchedly poor Mary Anne Geering from Sussex, on the English south coast. Her husband and sons were in a Benefit Society, and in September 1848 her husband died, followed to the grave in close succession by two of her sons. As each died, Mary Anne received money from the Society. Eventually, a local doctor grew suspicious when a third son fell ill and sent the boy's vomit to Professor Taylor. He found arsenic in it, and the boy was taken out of his mother's dubious care, ultimately saving his life. She was found to have bought arsenic seven times and the money she had received on each death was clearly the motive. In August 1849, she was found guilty of murder and hanged.

Her crimes added to the pile of other arsenic murders being discovered across the country at the time, another proof for *The Times* that arsenic sales should be regulated. But unlike in Essex, no ring of poisoners appeared to be operating in Sussex: Mary Anne Geering had been a lone agent. But could it be, as Bulwer-Lytton had suggested, that the newspaper publicity surrounding the Essex pantomime had planted the idea in her mind to poison her own family?

Lucky Hannah Southgate

Having successfully defended Hannah Southgate, towards the end of 1849 Ballantine defended another female accused of murder: the infamous Maria

Manning. Nicknamed 'The Bermondsey Horror', the crime was the brutal murder of Patrick O'Connor, and the alleged perpetrators were Maria and her husband Frederick. Cholera rampaged through Britain that year, claiming hundreds of thousands of lives. Bermondsey was one of the worst affected areas in London – by September, one in fifty-nine people in the area had died of the disease. In the middle of the epidemic, O'Connor disappeared, only to be found dead, in a makeshift burial under the floor of the Mannings' kitchen.

The case caught the public's imagination. Maria was Swiss, so had the glamorous allure of the 'foreigner'. She was, in some reports, beautiful, and had been lady's maid to aristocratic women. Just like Hannah Southgate in the pages of the *Ipswich Journal*, Maria's dress and appearance were described in fashion plate tones, earning mockery in *Punch* magazine. And there was sex: O'Connor had been Maria's lover before her marriage to Frederick and it seemed their relationship had continued. The 'electric telegraph' was used again in the Mannings' case, and led to Maria's arrest after she fled to Edinburgh. There was even a dramatic high seas pursuit when it was thought the Mannings were sailing to New York – alas, it turned out they weren't.

The Drunkard's Children, Plate V: 'From the bar of the gin-shop to the bar of the Old Bailey it is but one step', George Cruikshank, 1848.

The Mannings were both found guilty. Ballantine suspected that 'she was the power that really originated the deed of blood' and they were executed side by side. Their hanging attracted an enormous crowd, and Charles Dickens was among a group who had hired a nearby roof for ten guineas to get a good view. He was no stranger to seeing executions, but wrote how horrified he was that the crowd found entertainment in the hangings, rather than moral instruction.

In April 1850, Ballantine was dealing with a humdrum case of fraud at the Old Bailey. He was defending John Sadler, accused of defrauding an eating house keeper and his wife. In February 1850, the plaintiff, John Welham, had been living at Church Lane in Whitechapel. He owed £34 19s 6d to his landlord, Keats, and so he planned to move. On 7 February, Sadler was helping Welham to pack up his goods, which consisted of furniture, and the clothing of their children, lodgers and servants. Welham was able to pay his landlord £20, but Keats wanted a bill to insure payment of the remainder. Sadler offered to back the bill, and as the Welhams' household goods were to go into storage while they temporarily returned to East Anglia, Sadler offered to take their goods as security.

Amongst these goods was a looking-glass; Welham's wife was concerned it would get broken in Sadler's removal van.

'I will take this glass, if you please?' she said.

'No, ma'am,' Sadler replied. 'I desire you not to touch anything.'

'How is that?' Mrs Welham asked.

'I have got something in my pocket which will show you you are not to touch anything.'

A struggle ensued, but Mrs Welham managed to get the mirror, and carried it under her arm.

Sensing they were on the cusp of a fraud, they refused Sadler their belongings, so they were left in the van all night, the Welhams watching over it. The next morning, they were about to leave for the East Anglia Railway Station, but several men arrived and took the items from them by force. Welham claimed he had paid the money owed, and that Sadler would not return the goods, some of which he said Sadler had sold. They had gone to the magistrates, their servant indignant at Sadler having taken her clothing worth about £2, but she did not receive her items back. And Welham's wife was fined ten shillings for assault, which Sadler claimed had occurred during the struggle over the mirror.

Ballantine didn't realise who the 'comely middle-aged woman' married to Welham was, but the officer discreetly informed him that it was Hannah Southgate. How did Hannah feel when she realised the man who had saved her neck was now against her in court? Knowing his tough cross-examination technique, she must have wondered if he would reveal what he knew of her past in order to win the case for his client.

But, like a cat patting at a cornered mouse, after questioning Hannah about the goods – which she proudly (and inaccurately, considering the state of women's property rights at the time) said were hers, having bought them before her marriage with her own money – Ballantine questioned her about her husband's name. How long had he gone by the name Welham? Twelve months or more. And Hannah claimed he was born before his parents' marriage, hence he went by his mother's maiden name, although his father's name was Southgate. She admitted that she and John had married by the name of Southgate, and it was in spring the previous year that they had changed it to Welham. When John was cross-examined, he said they had changed the name when they moved to London, twelve months earlier – in other words, immediately after Hannah's acquittal.

Was John really illegitimate? His parents were married in February 1812 and he was baptised as John Southgate in May 1812. If he had been born before their marriage, they had waited until he was several months old before his baptism. John's mother had been born Mary Welham, but her father died when she was very young, and she took her stepfather's surname, Carter, so 'Welham' added an extra layer of disguise. Were John and Hannah pretending he was illegitimate in order to explain the reason for their pseudonym, hiding Hannah's past?

Sadler was found not guilty, but only because he was being charged for the wrong offence. He was detained until May 1850, when he could be tried for larceny, but the court decided the facts would not support a case of felony, and he was acquitted.

Catching up with the Southgates – or Welhams as they now called themselves – a year later in 1851, they were at Buxton Street in Mile End New Town. John was an eating house keeper, and 9-year-old Emily Ham, the only surviving child of Thomas and Hannah, lived with them. At the same address was Henry Harris and his family. Henry was an inspector of police. It is a great irony that a woman who stood trial for a poison murder helped to run a restaurant while living at the same address as a policeman: no wonder they went by an alias.

Back in Essex, Hannah had become a legend. In May 1849, only a few months after her trial, Mary Marson was walking along Wimpole Lane in Colchester. A gang of lads, led by 17-year-old Thomas Sadler, presumably no relative of the Whitechapel furniture thief, danced around her preventing her from passing. They yelled, '"Lucky Hannah Southgate", so as to lead any stranger who might have heard them, to believe that she was the woman tried at the last Essex Assize on a charge of wilful murder.' Anyone who had met Hannah is unlikely to have made that mistake, as Mary Marson was in her early fifties. She was, unfortunately for Thomas Sadler, the wife of the governor of Colchester's House of Correction: Mary may very well have known Hannah during her incarceration there. William Marson said he was 'determined not to let the matter rest' and Thomas was fined forty shillings plus expenses, or three months' imprisonment. Thomas, who came from a roguish family, knew very well it wasn't Hannah Southgate whom he encountered on Wimpole Lane, but enjoyed the opportunity to upset the matron of the House of Correction.

The phrase 'Lucky Hannah Southgate' persisted for some time. An inquest was opened in 1854 into the sudden death of Abraham Cutting. He had lived in Beaumont-cum-Moze, 5 miles east of Tendring through the twisting country lanes. Suspicions were aroused when his widow announced to everyone in the local pub that she was 'Lucky Hannah Southgate'. They went through their old dance steps again: the coroner, William Codd, opened the inquest, this time in Beaumont Hall rather than the pub. A body was exhumed and viscera sent to Professor Taylor. Taylor tested for arsenic, mercury, antimony and other mineral poisons but found nothing, and Codd said he placed little importance on what Abraham's widow had said: 'Anyone who had committed a murder would be very unlikely to blazon it forth in a tap-room.' Still, he had to defend the expense incurred by the inquest from the irate Essex ratepayers, and said the results of the post-mortem had justified the further step of Professor Taylor's analysis.

Yes, compared to Mary May, Hannah Southgate certainly had been lucky, even though she had to move away and live under an assumed name. And as it would turn out, she was luckier than Sarah Chesham, too.

Chapter 4

'English women are not to be trusted with arsenic'

On 16 May 1850, Richard Chesham died. He had been ill for several months, diagnosed with tuberculosis, that infamous Victorian killer that lurked in damp cottages. Had he been any other man in Clavering, he would have been mourned by his family and laid to rest. But this was the husband of Sarah Chesham: his death was automatically suspicious.

A post-mortem was performed on him four days later, and an inquest opened by C.C. Lewis, who had been the coroner at the Clavering and Manuden inquests back in 1846. The local relieving officer gave evidence that on 4 February 1850, Richard Chesham had applied for relief, allowing him a visit from a surgeon. He outlined the symptoms – Richard complained of pains in his chest and vomiting.

The surgeon who attended him was Stephen Clayton Hawkes; once again, he had been involved in the earlier cases, having administered medicine for James and Joseph Chesham. At Richard's post-mortem, he'd identified that the lungs were diseased, 'ulcerated and full of tubercules'. He had been visiting Richard for three or four weeks before he first complained of sickness. He got better, but sometimes the sickness would return, and finally the pain subsided and his symptoms were those of consumption once again. In Hawkes's opinion, Richard Chesham had died of tuberculosis. Another surgeon corroborated his testimony.

And it might have been left there, with a verdict of death by natural causes. As Hawkes had to defend himself from the press accusations when Sarah Chesham was tried three years earlier, he presumably would have been on his guard when called once again to their cottage. If he had thought there was anything suspicious about Richard's illness, he surely would have called in the police.

The author in The Fox and Hounds inn, Clavering.

But despite Sarah having been acquitted of those earlier poisonings, infamy still clung to her name, and the jury requested that Richard's viscera be sent to Professor Taylor. The press could scent another sensational story. Although the inquest was only reported locally, the newspapers began to stoke reader interest, for not only had Richard died, but 'the wretched woman has another son exceedingly ill.' This son was to be alluded to several times by the press, but was never named. As Sarah's initial trials in 1846 had involved the suspected murder of two of her sons, this ill son seemed to be evidence that she was slipping back into her old ways.

Towards the end of May, John Timewell Clarke, superintendent of police, had searched the Chesham's house, accompanied by PC John Pilley and his wife, Anne. Without female police officers, the searching of female suspects was down to policemen's wives. In a kneading trough in the Chesham's keeping room (or living room), Clarke found a small canvas bag containing about a pound of rice. They'd taken other items from her house but it was only the rice that Sarah protested about: she told them not to take it because it belonged to her father. Anne said she was standing nearby as Clarke took it; 'She seemed much excited and looked very wild at the time.'

It is hardly surprising that someone who had just lost their husband would be on edge, particularly someone who had gone through the ordeal of a triple murder trial only a few years before, and now had the police rummaging through her house again.

On 30 May, Essex was visited by a violent storm, 'the flashes of which were extremely vivid, being instantly followed by deafening peals of thunder.' Two stacks of wheat, ignited by 'electric fluid', burned in Great Waltham and the storm raged for two hours over Clavering. Trees were struck, and a cow left out in the fields was killed where it stood. Rain fell in torrents, swelling the streams that criss-cross the village, the water rising up to the cottage windowsills and washing the furniture out of the houses. Was this biblical deluge a divine judgment? News had arrived that Professor Taylor had found arsenic in Richard Chesham's remains.

The inquest was resumed in June. Clarke, corroborated by Anne Pilley, commented on Sarah's suspicious reaction to their removal of the bag of rice. But Sarah's father, James Parker, backed up his daughter, saying he'd bought the rice from Pavitt, the grocer, and had eaten some of it himself. He said Richard had laid ill in bed for some fourteen or fifteen weeks, and that he'd complained of his stomach, saying, 'he thought he had strained himself cutting chaff.'

Sarah Chesham was called and 'gave her evidence with little diffidence.' She said Richard had been healthy up until the last twelve months of his life, but 'about last Michaelmas he complained of a cough, as if from a cold.' He didn't get better, and continued to work until 'Old Christmas' – 6 January. He 'was taken ill with a pain in his shoulder, and at last it settled at the bottom of his body, and there it continued violently to pain him for nearly a fortnight.' For some days before his death he 'was like a raving madman with a pain in his stomach.' She said Richard had purged and vomited, from, she supposed, the medicine that Hawkes had given him. Aware of the emphasis that Clarke and Pilley had put on the rice, Sarah claimed she had never fed him with it. She gave him everything else *but* rice, she said.

The progress of his pain, along with Hawkes's medical evidence, suggests that Richard's tuberculosis had spread from his lungs into the abdomen. The predominant symptoms are abdominal pain, loss of appetite, weight loss, nausea, vomiting and diarrhoea. This sounds not unlike what Richard suffered, to the point that Willing, the relieving officer, later said that Richard looked like a skeleton. But no one ever suggested that his tuberculosis had spread, because vomiting, diarrhoea and abdominal pains are also symptoms of arsenic poisoning.

'I am going to ask you a question, and you may answer it, or not, as you please,' the coroner said. 'Have you had any poison, arsenic, in your house during the last six months?'

Sarah replied, 'I have not, and I can take my solemn oath that I never had any in my house, never during the whole of my life.'

'You lost two children?' the coroner asked.

'I lost two children from the use of arsenic,' Sarah said, 'but I did not know it until Mr Bowker told me so.' As Sarah had already been awaiting trial for the attempted poisoning of Solomon Taylor when her sons were exhumed, it seems that the discovery of arsenic in her sons had only reached her through her solicitor.

'Then you never had any poison?' the coroner reiterated.

'I have not seen any.' But then she added, 'My husband told me that he had some from Jim Parker some time since.'

'Since you have returned from Chelmsford,' the coroner continued, 'have you not made some statement about the children?'

'I said I was innocent of it.'

'Nothing to Mr Clarke the superintendent, or Pilley, the officer, about their being poisoned?'

'I said that Newport must have poisoned them; at least, I did not say that he poisoned them, but that he would be the death of them. That is all I said.'

There was sensation among the crowd, even though this accusation of Sarah's was no different from those she had made before.

Her father was called again, saying he couldn't imagine how arsenic got into the rice. He'd never seen any arsenic and didn't know what it looked like. Either he was telling the truth, or he was trying to protect his daughter, because next came Richard Chesham's mother, who would contradict what Sarah had said.

Whereas Sarah had claimed that her husband had eaten no rice at all, on the contrary, his mother, who had attended occasionally during his illness, said she had seen Sarah give him rice several times. The last time was about four days before his death. And she added, if Sarah said 'that she had not given him any, she had told an untruth.'

Now came the star witness, the forensic expert himself: Professor Alfred Swaine Taylor, called once again to rural Essex. The report of his analysis was lengthy. He had found patches of red inflammation in Richard's stomach, and following his usual tests, had discovered arsenic, 'but in such small quantities as to prevent him stating positively that the poison was the cause of death.' He had only found one twenty-fifth of a grain (about 2.6mg) of arsenic.

But not so the bag of rice. This, he said, contained from 12 to 16 grains (780–1,040mg) of arsenic. 'It was mixed in the rice like a powder, and to a casual observer might appear like flour. There was sufficient to kill six persons.' Taylor had to explain how the rice could contain so much arsenic, but the body so little. He suggested that it had been administered in small doses, a process known as 'slow poisoning'. 'If a small dose was taken a week before death, the greater part might be carried away by urine and secretion, so

Professor Alfred Swaine Taylor, photographed by Ernest Edwards, 1868.

as to leave only a small part in the body.' Small doses would have accelerated Richard's death – 'where there were consumptive symptoms they would tend to weaken the bodily power' and would 'excite great pain and anguish, and debilitate and exhaust the patient.'

Local woman Hannah Phillips was brought in. She said that at the last harvest, she had seen Sarah crying about her children being poisoned, which to most people would seem to be evidence of Sarah's continuing, unstaunchable grief. But then Hannah's evidence took a turn into darkness: she alleged Sarah told her that she'd had some arsenic, and she'd hidden it in a tree stump. And after the first meeting of the inquest, Sarah had urged Hannah not to say anything about the poison. She claimed Sarah had said, 'It was not worthwhile to say any more about it, her trouble was quite enough, and that was an old grievance.' And then Sarah said she was wrong about the tree stump, but she had hidden the arsenic somewhere else.

Sarah's cousin, another James Parker, said that about four years ago, he had bought two ounces of arsenic for Richard Chesham. The coroner was not happy about this, and asked why he hadn't mentioned it at the previous inquests. James replied that he 'thought it alluded to the woman' – it was Richard he'd bought it for, not Sarah. The coroner said he could be indicted for perjury – but this would have been a misstep, because the Chesham boys died in January 1845. How could they have been poisoned by arsenic that wasn't bought until a year later?

Now it came time for the coroner to pass the case on to the jury. He remarked that it was difficult to say how the poison had been administered, and the evidence of Richard's mother complicated matters. Apparently referring to the illness of Sarah's son, 'this difficulty and complication might tend to impede the ends of justice in another case which might arise.' But the jury, having consulted for half an hour, were satisfied with Hawkes's original medical evidence. Richard Chesham, they decided, had died of 'tubercular consumption, the evidence failing to prove that the arsenic found in the body had accelerated death.'

But the coroner was suspicious: he passed it on to the magistrates, believing that Sarah could be proceeded against for administering poison with intent.

Palmer, Smethurst and the fallibility of Professor Taylor

The case slipped out of the newspapers for a few months. Sarah had not been charged with any crime, and her son recovered. Had he been labouring under symptoms of arsenic poisoning, it would have been wise for anything he brought up to have been sent to Professor Taylor for analysis, as had happened with the son of Mary Ann Geering, but it wasn't.

Taylor was greatly admired in his day, particularly in the 1840s, even though ratepayers might complain of his costs each time he was embroiled in a mysterious death. But as the 1850s wore on, people began to doubt the apparently omniscient powers of forensic science, and this was partly due to Taylor's involvement in two trials, both involving medical men accused of poisoning.

In 1856, William Palmer, 'the Rugeley Poisoner', was on trial for murder. He was a member of the Royal College of Surgeons but was more attracted to horse racing and was soon in massive debt. He insured the life of his wife for a huge sum of money, and she died mysteriously soon afterwards. In 1855, he insured his brother's life, and two days later, Palmer bought prussic acid from a chemist; his brother then died. John Cook, a friend of Palmer's, won at the Shrewsbury races and went for a drink with Palmer that evening. He fell ill, but recovered. A few days later, he went for a coffee with Palmer, and fell ill again. He recovered when Palmer went away to London, where the doctor bought strychnine and opium. When Cook met Palmer again, Cook once more became ill and swiftly died. The agonising cramps he suffered resembled the symptoms of tetanus, which are the same as those produced by strychnine poisoning.

Palmer behaved suspiciously, arranging Cook's burial without his family's presence, and the winnings had disappeared. Suspicions were raised, and Cook's death was investigated. Palmer interfered at every step, being present at the post-mortem, and then jostled the doctor so that Cook's stomach contents were spilt. The jar containing the stomach temporarily disappeared, and was found with tampered seals. Palmer bribed the pot boy at the inn where the post-mortem was performed to upset the cart that was carrying the jars to London.

Professor Taylor received the jars and, unsurprisingly, found that the stomach contents had vanished. He was unable to find strychnine but did identify antimony, although not enough to kill. The symptoms of antimony are not the same as those of strychnine, but still Taylor claimed it was strychnine that had killed Cook, even though he hadn't found any in the viscera he tested. The inquest jury were convinced of Palmer's guilt and he was found guilty of murder. Palmer's wife and brother were exhumed and Taylor found that she had been poisoned with antimony. He was unable to find any poison in Palmer's brother, but still stated that he had been poisoned, and the inquest jury agreed with him.

But Taylor was criticised for his handling of the evidence, especially as, before the trial, he had spoken about his analyses in the press. Because the trial was based heavily on scientific evidence, Taylor's inability to find strychnine became a problem, but still Palmer was hanged. On the gallows, Palmer said, 'Cook did not die from strychnine.' Was this a roundabout confession? He said no more and took the secret to his grave.

Four years later, Professor Taylor was called on as the scientific witness when Dr Smethurst was accused of murdering his wealthy wife, Isabella, whom he had bigamously wed. There was a clear financial motive for her murder and it was thought he had poisoned her. Isabella's symptoms were those of poisoning, and while she still lived, one of her 'evacuations' was given to Professor Taylor to test. He found a deposit, either arsenic or antimony. After she died, he tested her viscera, as well as various pills and potions found in her bedroom. He could find no arsenic in her body, but did find a small amount in a bottle containing chlorate of potash (potassium chlorate), and gave this as evidence at the police court hearing.

But by the time the case went to trial in July 1859, Taylor realised he'd made a mistake. The copper gauze that was an essential part of the Reinsch test for arsenic had, in fact, contained arsenic. The chlorate of potash had dissolved the gauze, and he had added more and more gauzes, all of which dissolved. As he saw it, the copper gauze didn't release the arsenic it contained until it met the corrosive liquid he was testing.

The jury still found Dr Smethurst guilty of murdering Isabella, but Taylor's mistake led to a war of words in *The Times*, with various people chiming in to say they thought his error meant that the scientific evidence in the trial should be thrown out entirely. Petitions were sent to the Secretary of State, and Smethurst was pardoned and saved from the gallows. Taylor's reputation was dented. William Ballantine, the barrister who had successfully defended Hannah Southgate, had been retained by Isabella's family to prosecute. He felt there was still abundant evidence to support Smethurst's conviction, and he was glad the doctor finally saw the inside of a cell when he was imprisoned for twelve months for bigamy. Ballantine remarked in his memoirs that it was 'a series of blunders' showing 'the danger of placing too great reliance upon scientific testimony'.

With these cases in mind, we might look at the scientific evidence produced against Sarah Chesham in 1850 and wonder just how watertight it was. During the Smethurst debacle, Taylor claimed he had used the copper gauze 'for a great many years, and never before discovered the presence of arsenic in it.' He said he would continue to use it unless he had to test chlorate of potash again. But it does raise a worrying question – although Taylor said he'd tested them before making the analyses to make sure they were pure, clearly some of them weren't. And just how corrosive would a substance have to be to release arsenic from copper? Would the acidic contents of the human stomach, which includes potassium chlorate as well as hydrochloric acid and sodium chloride, be sufficient to release arsenic? And hydrochloric acid was an integral part of the Reinsch test anyway. If this is so, then there has to be some doubt about the very tiny amount of arsenic that he found inside Richard Chesham – that the arsenic came, not from anything ingested by the dead man, but from contaminated materials used by Taylor in his analysis.

No one commented on the possibility that Richard Chesham had been suffering from abdominal tuberculosis, and it was Taylor who cut into the stomach and intestines to analyse them. He saw red patches of inflammation, which he attributed to the arsenic he had found, but could there have been visible signs of abdominal tuberculosis in those organs that Taylor simply didn't see, because he wasn't looking for them?

Then comes the issue of the rice. Taylor was clear that there was so much arsenic in it, it was visible to the eye. But it's a very curious piece of evidence. Sarah's panic at seeing Clarke remove the rice from the house was attributed to her fear that it was to be analysed, but at what point did Clarke and Pilley know that Taylor had found arsenic in it? If they knew before the inquest, it's quite possible that in their verbal testimony, they exaggerated Sarah's reaction, knowing what Taylor had discovered. She had just lost her husband, and aside from any fears she might have had that she was about to be accused of murder, she may well have been thinking about her household budget and was unhappy at the loss of their food.

If she had poisoned Richard by lacing the rice with arsenic, why did she leave it in the kneading trough in the living room? The house was full of people – her father was living there along with her three remaining sons, as well as Harriet, her daughter, and presumably Harriet's husband, Nathan Chipperfield. Surely it would be dangerous to keep the rice hanging about, and as her father had bought it, surely there was a danger he would eat some of it. Or might the pitiless 'murderess-for-hire' from *The Times*'s leaders come to mind, and we assume that she didn't care if anyone accidentally dropped off short from white powder in her house?

Once the deed was done and Richard had died, why would she have kept the poisoned rice in her house and not destroyed it? Of course, a genius criminal like Moriarty is not often found outside the pages of fiction, but hanging on to such an incriminating piece of evidence stretches credulity.

Perhaps the arsenic got into the rice by accident. Certainly this was the case with the poisoning of a whole family in Gislingham, Suffolk in 1835, which resulted in two deaths and illness for the rest of the household. Some arsenic stored by their lodger accidentally fell into the family's supply of flour – he had thoughtlessly kept it on a shelf above the flour sack.

But what if the arsenic had been planted in the rice to incriminate Sarah?

We might suspect anyone from Clavering who believed that justice had not been done in 1847, or we might home in on particular people: the police. It's possible that her acquittal had caused embarrassment to the authorities, especially once Mary May and Hannah Southgate were paraded before the public. *The Times*'s fondness for alluding to Sarah and skewing the facts must have caused a great deal of discussion behind closed doors in the north-west corner of Essex. C.C. Lewis had been the coroner at the inquests in 1846; finding himself four years later investigating another suspicious death involving Sarah Chesham may have forced him to override the jury's verdict and press for her prosecution. The expense of her prosecution that led to an acquittal had not gone down well with the ratepayers of the county, and perhaps this time they wanted to make sure she couldn't escape.

Accusing the police of planting evidence might seem rather strong, but the Essex Constabulary had been formed only ten years earlier; police procedure was still being developed. They were set up initially as a preventative force, and procedures for investigation were still in their infancy: it was not unknown for the police to manipulate evidence.

The infamous murder of a small child at Road Hill House in Somerset in 1860 would have been solved quickly by Inspector Whicher, when he was called in by Scotland Yard, had a vital clue not vanished. He suspected the murderer to be the child's half-sister, Constance Kent, aged sixteen at the time. It took a confession by Constance some years later for Whicher to be proved right, and at that point the local police (Somerset Constabulary had only been created in 1856) admitted that they had destroyed a bloodied nightdress. It was strongly felt Victorian decency that forced them to this end, concerned that the blood was a young lady's menstrual fluid, which could not be put under public scrutiny. It says a lot about the Victorian mindset concerning class and gender that such a key piece of evidence was suppressed. Therefore, it does not seem entirely unlikely that the Clavering police, in 1850, had planted arsenic in the Cheshams' bag of rice.

There is want of that strong medical proof

C.C. Lewis, the Essex police and the magistrates were kept busy over the summer, investigating Richard Chesham's death. They carefully kept their investigations secret from the newspapers. Today, this bundle of papers can be viewed in the reading room of The National Archives in Kew: it shines a light on the way that justice was sought at this period.

They approached Professor Taylor, who said he thought it unlikely Sarah would be convicted under administering poison with intent. The case, he believed, stood 'too much upon presumption' and although he felt there was little doubt that arsenic had caused Richard's bouts of illness, 'there is a want of that strong <u>medical proof</u> which is necessary for conviction.' (Emphasis in original.)

The magistrates had been questioning people behind closed doors, particularly Hannah Phillips, who had come forward with more information. She alleged that about two years earlier, the Cheshams, with Sarah's elderly parents, had moved to a cottage near hers. The two women became friendly, Sarah always asking Hannah to visit her house. Hannah said that Sarah was uneasy, and kept saying that Thomas Newport had sent her to poison Lydia

Taylor's child. She claimed Sarah admitted to poisoning Solomon Taylor, and that Thomas Newport had poisoned Sarah's sons. But Hannah didn't explain why – what possible motive did Thomas have for murdering James and Joseph Chesham? And why did Sarah, if what Hannah said was true, poison Solomon Taylor – what hold did Thomas have over her? Was he paying her or threatening her? Hannah did not say, and this makes her evidence look like mean-minded gossip, based on what would have been spread about Clavering by those who disagreed with Sarah's original acquittals.

Hannah had something to say about Richard Chesham's illness. Last harvest, Sarah had told Hannah to do as she had done – go to the butcher and buy a sheep's head, boil the liver and 'lights' (offal), cut them up and put them into mince pies, then take them to Sarah's house and she would season it for her, because 'there was no sin in killing husbands such as theirs.' Hannah didn't elaborate on what this meant – the implication is that the seasoning would be poison, and the magistrates believed she meant they both had sickly husbands who couldn't earn a decent wage. Hannah claimed Sarah had made such pies for her husband and son, and given them to eat in the harvest field; they had lived mainly on those pies and on rice. This seems retro-fitted around Taylor's discovery of arsenic in the rice.

No motive for poisoning Richard had been alleged at the inquest, but now Hannah presented one: 'Sarah Chesham told her times and times that she would not live with her husband for there was another man wanted her and was ready to receive her when she came out of Chelmsford Gaol. Other witnesses can prove Sarah Chesham lived unhappily with her husband.' Hannah didn't name him, but they might have suspected this man to be Thomas Newport, with whom Sarah had been seen before; the insinuation had been that they were conducting an affair. Newport was further implicated when Hannah said she hadn't come forward with the full story before because her husband worked for John Newport, Thomas's brother, and she was scared he would lose his job. When her husband heard that Sarah had instigated Hannah to kill him, he wished his wife to tell the truth – and now she did.

In August, the magistrates referred the case to a barrister at the Middle Temple, Henry Hawkins (who would go on to become a judge). He had assisted with Thomas Newport's defence when he stood trial in 1847.

The magistrates told him this was the only evidence they had, and asked, somewhat desperately, if there was sufficient to apprehend Sarah for poisoning or attempting to poison, and if so, under what statute. And if there wasn't enough evidence, was there some other offence they could charge her with? And they asked him for general advice on how they should act.

Hawkins said the case was fit for the consideration of a jury, even if he couldn't promise that a conviction could be obtained. He advised that Sarah be arrested at once, because he didn't think that more evidence would 'be brought to light by suffering her to remain at large.'

Because of Taylor's belief that there wasn't enough medical evidence, Hawkins didn't see how it 'can very well be mended.' He advised careful examination of the 'medical gentlemen'. They should trace Richard's stomach carefully through each hand it passed on the way to Taylor, presumably to prevent anyone claiming it had been tampered with to incriminate Sarah.

And there was the matter of how the arsenic had been acquired. Hawkins thought 'it is a matter of some importance to discover if possible whether Newport did at or about the time of the deaths of the children purchase any arsenic, and I would cause these enquiries to be made throughout the neighbourhood of Clavering, and also at the various towns where Newport was in the habit of attending either at market or for other purposes.' This was required so they could corroborate Hannah Phillips's testimony.

It was an incredibly onerous task – the boys had died nearly six years earlier, and a busy, prosperous farmer like Newport would have had business in many places around Essex and in neighbouring counties. Anyone could walk into a shop and buy arsenic, so how could they expect a shopkeeper to specifically remember Newport buying it five years before? And even if someone was willing to swear that he had, Newport could easily claim he'd been using it on his farm. He'd even admitted to possessing arsenic at Sarah Chesham's first trial.

But they had to take care and make their enquiries first before they approached him, 'for it is not difficult to see that by examining him at once subsequent enquiry might prove unavailing.'

The provenance of the rice had to be proved; had her father really bought it for himself? However, Hawkins felt that even if it was her father's, she still had access to it so it remained a useful piece of evidence. They had to prove that she prepared all of Richard's food, particularly in his last forty-eight hours, as this would probably be when Taylor would claim that tiny quantity he found had been ingested. Witnesses would be required to testify Richard's symptoms in the early stage of his illness, and he also advised them to find out if Sarah had recently bought arsenic.

He observed that they needed to keep publicity to a minimum, which explains why it was kept out of the papers, 'for too great publicity might possibly stifle an investigation already requiring great care and attention.'

The magistrates forwarded their evidence and Hawkins' suggestions to the Secretary of State. They asked that the government would pay for the costs of investigating, because 'there is no person willing to undertake the responsibility of the prosecution.' The Attorney and Solicitor General's office replied on 21 August 1850, saying they couldn't promise to cover the costs, but urged that further investigation should take place. They recommended that Sarah be interviewed again by the magistrates, and her father should be asked about the ownership of the rice. 'Care should however be taken not to let him know beforehand on what point he is to be examined.' And they said they should find the tree stump where Sarah had, according to Hannah, hidden arsenic, and it should be analysed for any traces of the poison. One wonders what Professor Taylor made of that.

This already notorious woman

In early September, Sarah Chesham found herself in handcuffs again, and was taken to a cell in Newport police station. The story could at last appear in the press.

The Times went with 'Extraordinary murders by poisoning at Clavering' and told their readers it was an 'extraordinary and fearful system of poisoning, which has excited so much alarm throughout this part of the country'. After Sarah's original acquittal, they said there had 'been much gossip about the poisoning, and "how bad husbands could be got rid of",' which sounds as if they were conflating Sarah with Hannah Southgate. They claimed Richard had been 'a healthy sort of man', downplaying the evidence that he had died of tuberculosis, and at the inquest there had been 'a vast amount of prevarication, with a view apparently to screen the guilty party'.

The magistrates were 'resolved upon making an effort to solve the mystery' and 'the conduct of different persons was watched.' They printed Hannah Phillips's evidence about the 'seasoned' pie, but left out mention of her fear that her husband would lose his job with Thomas Newport's brother. Hannah had been ill-treated by her husband, hence Sarah suggesting that she should poison him. 'She would not have lived with her husband if he had treated her in the same way.' This is clearly not the same as the evidence written up by the magistrates; the motive was thought to be the husbands' ill health.

The Times said that while Hannah gave evidence, Sarah had looked uneasy, and she finally said 'she could tell the truth as well as Mrs Phillips.' According to Sarah, it was Hannah who had approached her, asking for a 'poisoned pill' to kill her husband.

From 'The Hours of the Night', *Illustrated Exhibitor & Magazine of Art*, 1852.

This puts an intriguing slant on Hannah's involvement in the case. *The Times* had said that the people of Clavering saw Sarah as a murderess-for-hire – even if this hadn't been true, the locals may have come to believe it thanks to the press. It is possible that Hannah wanted to poison her own husband and had approached Sarah, thinking she would help her. When the inquest opened into Richard's death, Hannah may have panicked and flipped the truth around, in case Sarah told the authorities of her request. By adding various unprovable 'facts', such as Sarah hiding the arsenic under a tree stump, Hannah could conceal her own guilt.

The local papers carried the story on the following day, their reports largely the same as that in *The Times*, presumably because it had the same source, although the *Essex Standard* explained she was being arrested under the poison element of the Offences Against the Person Act of 1837:

> Whoever shall attempt to administer to any person any poison, &c., with intent to commit murder, although no injury be effected, shall be deemed guilty of felony, and shall be liable to be transported for life, or not less than fifteen years, or imprisoned for three years.

This is the same Act under which Emma Elizabeth Hume was convicted in 1847 for attempting to poison her husband with sugar of lead.

At the end of September, Sarah was brought before the magistrates again at Newport police station. Hannah Phillips gave evidence, further embroidering her tale. She claimed Sarah told her that Thomas Newport had given Joseph and James Chesham a halfpenny each, and that these had been put in their coffin with them, and that Newport had wanted Sarah to poison Lydia Taylor as well as her baby; Newport was allegedly angry with Sarah because she refused to do so. Hannah mentioned the 'seasoned' pies again, and the magistrates asked her why she had held back. She said her husband worked for Mr Newport, 'and she was told that if she stated more than she had Mrs Chesham would be sent to Chelmsford.' She said Sarah informed her 'she had not wit enough to poison her husband as she had,' and denied she had approached Sarah for a poisoned pill.

About a week after the inquest was opened, Hannah shouted 'Sally Arsenic' at Sarah as she passed by in the street, saying Sarah had poisoned her husband. Sarah replied, 'You might have done it,' as if Hannah could have poisoned her own husband, and Hannah replied, 'No, you wretch!'

Hannah's somewhat yobbish behaviour, yelling at a newly widowed woman in the street, does not recommend her as a good witness.

Amongst other witnesses who had spoken before was PC Pilley, with more evidence that he hadn't given earlier. However, the coroner's questions to Sarah at the second meeting of the inquest imply he had already passed it on. He alleged that when Sarah came back from the assize in 1847, 'she stated that the lawyers had informed her she could not be hurt for what she had been tried for, and that she would tell them all about it.' This is the procedural defence of double jeopardy, where someone cannot be retried for the same offence. Pilley claimed Sarah had said 'that Newport had given her children the poison in a peppermint-drop, and that he gave them something to take it' – this presumably is the half-pennies that Hannah Phillips had mentioned. And Pilley said Sarah admitted that Newport had given her a bottle to give to Lydia Taylor: the contents were not disclosed in the paper, but the implication was clear – Sarah had come back from Chelmsford, admitting to the crimes for which she had been acquitted.

Or had she? If Pilley wasn't telling untruths, recall how forceful Sarah had been in her belief that Newport had murdered her children. She may have made these allegations believing herself to be protected by double jeopardy, in order to incriminate the man she believed had killed her sons. Why would children need to be bribed to swallow sweets? What motive was there for Newport, or indeed Sarah, to murder Joseph and James? And the bottle she said Newport intended for Lydia may have been Sarah's fib, intended to implicate Newport: unfortunately this was now being used to incriminate herself.

Similar evidence was given by John Holgate, who was a shoemaker from Debden, 7 miles east of Clavering. He said he'd been to Sarah's house, and that she had cried, 'and said that Newport had been the ruin of her, and that he ought to have been hanged, for he had killed her two children' and she 'spoke of what he had given those at Manuden; and he said that he would tell her after she had done it.'

Sarah's cousin, James, was interviewed again about the arsenic he had given Richard. When he heard that Joseph and James had been poisoned, he spoke to Richard about it, who told him that it couldn't have been the poison

James got for him as he had already used it all. James was also employed by one of the Newports, who told him not to say anything about it.

Thomas Newport, unsurprisingly, stated that he'd never given poison or arsenic to Sarah, or any of her family. When James Parker junior 'had told him that he had got a two-penny worth of arsenic,' Thomas replied, 'Don't say anything to me about it, say it before the coroner.' He denied telling James to keep silent about it. He did, however, admit to using arsenic 'to dress wheat for a certain piece of land some years back.'

Professor Taylor was present again and repeated his evidence, then the magistrates decided to commit Sarah for trial at the next assize 'for feloniously administering to the deceased a certain poison, with intent to kill and murder.'

Sarah was told she could now make a statement, and she said that she was innocent, 'and she wished they would take her before a witch, and then they would know who poisoned her husband.' Witches being thin on the ground in mid-nineteenth-century Essex, this was presumably not done. Some of her children were allowed in to see her before she was taken away; she took off her rings and gave them to her daughter.

All of the witnesses were bound in £20 each to appear at the assize, except Thomas Newport, who was bound in £100; whether because he was wealthy or because they felt his evidence was of great importance isn't clear.

The Doddinghurst Murder

Sarah Chesham vanished from the newspapers, overshadowed when Thomas Drory was accused of murder in October 1850. He was the 20-year-old son of a farmer from Doddinghurst, 12 miles south-east of Chelmsford. The crime had overtones of the infamous 1827 'Red Barn Murder' in Polstead, Suffolk, when William Corder, a farmer's son, shot dead his pregnant lover, Maria Marten. Drory had seduced Jael Denny, a local girl of humble status, and left her pregnant, not unlike Thomas Newport had Lydia Taylor. Unlike Newport, Drory had strangled Jael and left her to die. Jael, named after an Old Testament woman who kills a man by driving a tent peg through his skull, was nine months' pregnant; she was a few days from giving birth.

Drory protested his innocence in the face of overwhelming evidence. Even Professor Taylor was involved, examining Drory's 'small clothes' –

Horrible and Bar-bar-ous Murder of Poor
JAEL DENNY,
THE ILL-FATED VICTIM OF THOMAS DRORY.

An example of 'street art', this garish engraving of the Doddinghurst murder was for sale on the London streets. From Mayhew's *London Labour and the London Poor*.

his knee breeches – worn on the night of Jael's death for spots of blood. Forensic science was not yet so evolved for him to state whose blood it was; blood type analysis would not be possible until the early twentieth century, and DNA analysis of blood had to wait for Alec Jeffreys' discovery of DNA fingerprinting in 1984. However, Taylor believed he could still confidently claim that the spots were blood and not some other substance, even though he couldn't differentiate between animal and human blood.

Taylor believed that some of the spots had been wetted and wiped, which could indicate a guilty party trying to remove them, but no attempt had been made to wash the breeches. He was able to identify the spots as blood, because although many substances could leave a red stain on fabric, only blood would leave a clot as it stained. As clots could only be formed by newly shed blood, these were the breeches of a murderer.

The presence of blood from the strangulation indicated how violent the attack on Jael had been, and it ruled out the idea that she had strangled herself. The inquest jury took only ten minutes to return a verdict of wilful murder and Thomas Drory was taken to Springfield Gaol, to wait six months for the next assize.

A week of horrors

In February 1851, the *Essex Standard* printed a list of 'the more flagrant offences' of the sixty-five prisoners to be tried at the Spring Assize in Chelmsford. Drory headed the list, followed by four other alleged murderers and twelve cases of arson (one of which involved another relative of this author). Quite far down the list was Sarah Chesham, for attempted murder, and after her came a shooting with intent to kill at Saffron Walden, manslaughter on the Eastern Counties' Railway, embezzlement and forgery in Maldon, bigamy in Braintree, and somewhat pitifully, a man from Great Dunmow who had tried to strangle himself.

On Thursday, 6 March, Sarah Chesham was led once more into the dock at Chelmsford Shire Hall. Liberal politician Lord Chief Justice Campbell was the judge, and William Henry Bodkin, with Mr Clerk, prosecuted. Without counsel herself, Sarah was left entirely undefended.

She was not Hannah Southgate; she did not have a wealthy husband who could retain a barrister like William Ballantine. Charles Chadwick Jones, Serjeant–at–Law, who had saved her neck before, but without similar success for Mary May, could not help her. A year earlier, Jones was taken to the Insolvent Debtors Court, owing £9,000. He was in extremely bad health, to the extent that he had a 'medical gentleman' attending him in court. The creditors gave evidence: he owed large sums of unpaid rent and unpaid bills to a grocer and cheesemonger, and a man from whom he had bought window blinds. Jones said he had been promised some committee business in Parliament by a relative of his wife, but it wasn't fulfilled. He was expecting money from his professional work, and was owed £1,000 by solicitors. When he took the coif, becoming a Serjeant–at–Law, it had cost him £400, but soon afterwards an Act was passed that diminished the value of the coif and halved his income.

The pressure of his debts only served to worsen Jones's illness, to the point that he could not work, and he died in 1852, having been ill for three years. *Bell's Life* claimed his death 'was brought on by mental suffering.' Even if he had wanted to defend Sarah again, he simply could not.

It is possible that the Essex magistrates' concerns about the expense of prosecuting Sarah meant they were unwilling to pay for her defence, and no charitable donations came her way to help her. As the charge did not carry the death sentence, they may have felt they could sidestep her having a defence counsel, even though, when Emma Elizabeth Hume had been charged with the same offence in 1847, the judge had criticised the county for economising and employing no counsel on either side. But this time, Lord Justice Campbell didn't pass comment.

The *Chelmsford Chronicle* gave little space to the trial as the 'evidence has already appeared in our columns.' The *Essex Standard* went through the witnesses one by one, but it was *The Times* that reported Sarah's trial in greatest detail; after all, over the years, they had evinced great fascination with her. She was, they said, 'a masculine-looking woman', altered from her first trial, where they had described her as 'a good-looking woman'. Had the strain of the years paid a heavy toll on her looks, or were only innocent women attractive?

Referring back to Sarah's trials of 1847, *The Times* claimed that the evidence had 'left very little doubt of her guilt' – clearly not what the juries had thought, as they had acquitted her. To tie her in with the other poisoning cases that the county was known for, and to reinforce *The Times*'s wholly invented idea that Essex was home to a 'system of poisoning', they stated that Mary May 'admitted after her conviction that she had been instigated' by Sarah to become a poisoner herself. There were no grounds for this claim whatsoever: the local Essex papers had been clear that May made no confession before her execution. Besides, the idea that two near-illiterate women living on opposite sides of Essex could have been acquaintances, let alone swapped poisoning tips as part of a murder network, stretches credulity.

In the intervening months since the inquest, Willing, the relieving officer, had died; his testimony was read out in court. Willing had said that on one occasion when he had visited Richard, 'he showed him his body, which appeared swollen to nearly double its ordinary size, and his arms and legs appeared like those of a skeleton.'

Hawkes, the surgeon, had changed his tune. Whereas at the inquest he said that Richard had died of tuberculosis, he now said that 'all of the symptoms were such as would be the result of the administration of small doses of some irritant poison.' Was he aligning his testimony to match the eminent professor's findings, to prevent criticism of his medical ability? He said Sarah had come to him 'in a very angry manner' while Richard was ill, because a post-mortem would be performed if he died. This would appear suspicious, but it isn't unusual for people to dislike the thought of their loved one's remains being interfered with. Without defence counsel, Sarah, who had been in prison since September, asked her own questions. They were not printed in the paper, but from the answers given by Hawkes, it appears she asked him if he remembered visiting Richard in the February, and if he observed any bruises on his body. Hawkes did remember visiting him, and prescribing him medicine 'and a piece of wet rag to place upon his body'. He 'did not observe an appearance of a bruise or hurt' upon him.

The surgeon who carried out the post-mortem with Hawkes gave evidence, and the only question Sarah seems to have asked him was who had fetched the bladder that the stomach contents were placed in. It appears to be a desperate attempt to suggest that it had been tampered with in order to frame her.

Superintendent Clarke reported his search of Sarah's house and taking away the rice; all Sarah asked him was, did he have a warrant? No, he did not.

There was some debate with the judge and Bodkin as to whether or not they could admit Sarah's testimony given at the inquest; she had not been charged and cautioned at the time, and she didn't have a defence counsel who could make the case for it not to be put in. Eventually, they decided that it could be read. 'The most material part of the statement,' *The Times* said, 'was that the prisoner denied positively ever having given the deceased any rice.'

Professor Taylor was carefully questioned, emphasising the idea of Richard having been poisoned by small doses over many days. Taylor added that when he was examined at Sarah's last trials, he had 'in her presence, described the nature of arsenic and its mode of action.' *The Times*, in its leader the next day, used this to emphasise her gratuitous criminality, 'the woman, then in peril of her life, stood quietly at the bar, listened, and learnt. No sooner was she discharged than she availed herself of her lesson.' They could not prove this was true, but published it anyway. In fact, while Sarah awaited trial in 1847, the *Essex Standard* had printed an extract from the

Medical Gazette, which possibly emanated from Professor Taylor's pen, about slow poisoning. Had Sarah wanted to learn how to poison, just as Bulwer–Lytton said, she had only to consult a newspaper.

Sarah's father gave evidence about his rice, and Henry Prooth, a grocer's assistant in Clavering, proved that James had, indeed, bought some rice from him, about three weeks before Richard's death. No one, however, proved where the arsenic had come from, but by this point it didn't matter, because Hannah Phillips took the stand.

She repeated what she had said before, enlarging on certain aspects, claiming Sarah had quarrelled with her husband. No answers were published to any questions by Sarah – it appears she did not cross-examine Hannah at all. An experienced barrister could have torn Hannah's evidence apart; Ballantine would have taken sadistic pleasure in questioning her about her own marriage, and could very well have turned the tide of the trial. But there was no Ballantine, no skilled cross-examiner: Hannah Phillips's testimony went unchallenged, and put a noose around her neighbour's neck.

Two other Clavering locals, who had not appeared at the inquests, gave evidence: a labourer who claimed he had seen Richard complain of stomach pain after eating one of Sarah's 'seasoned' pies, and a woman who claimed Sarah had made various comments about poison, including a threat to poison Hannah Phillips. Professor Taylor was recalled and asked by the prosecution if the symptoms reported by the labourer were those of arsenic poison. Yes, they were, Professor Taylor said. There was no defence counsel to ask him if the symptoms could have had any other cause.

Finally came Sarah's own 'long rambling statement'. She said she was innocent, and that any poison found inside her husband must have come from things that people had been giving him constantly while he was ill. She denied all knowledge of it, and complained that she had been unable to produce witnesses – being illiterate and in prison, preparing her own defence must have been all but impossible. 'She protested that she had at all times treated her husband with the greatest kindness, and that the principal portion of the evidence was adduced against her from a feeling of spite and revenge.'

The jury returned their verdict of guilty almost immediately. While the Offences Against the Persons Act of 1837 allowed for a punishment of transportation or imprisonment, the judge put on the black cap and sentenced

Sarah to death. He agreed with the verdict and thought the evidence overpowering – a startling admission when the lack of hard evidence nearly prevented Sarah from being arrested in the first place, but the fear that she had escaped justice before weighed heavily on the verdict. The judge said he feared it wasn't the first time she had killed and 'there would be no safety for mankind' if punishment did not follow her guilt. *The Times* reported the judge saying Sarah had confessed to killing her two children, which appears to be an error, either of the judge or the reporter.

The Times portrayed her as cold and unfeeling to the last, reporting that Sarah left the dock with a firm step. The *Essex Standard*, echoing its report of Mary May's sentencing, said the judge was 'so affected that he could barely proceed; and when the prisoner was removed many ladies sitting upon the bench were bathed in tears.'

After the Chelmsford trials, Lord Campbell went to Lewes to preside at the Spring Assize there. Mentioning his experience in Essex, he said, 'I had a week of horrors.' The *Chelmsford Chronicle* rushed to defend the county. They protested at the idea that in Essex 'our population is brutalised and our poor neglected' – they pointed to the number of schools and places of worship that were being built in the county. They blamed, instead, lack of employment and bad wages, and pointed to Drory – who had been found guilty of Jael Denny's murder and was sentenced to death – and Chesham as aberrations. Mirroring *The Times*'s assessment of her, they said Chesham followed murder 'as a pastime and trade'.

Drory had confessed to his crime while awaiting his execution: the fact that Sarah did not had the press accuse her of callousness, rather than wonder if she really was guilty at all. And they printed what the prison governor would later point out was an untruth: she 'distinctly admits that she has taken off several persons by arsenic.'

The Times's leading article, published the day after they reported Sarah's trial, repeated many errors they had printed about her before, that she had 'led a notorious and almost public career for four years' following her acquittal, that she was 'a professed murderess in her own neighbourhood, and that mothers locked their children up when she was seen about the premises.' Whereas Sarah had been accused of putting a 'sucker' in Solomon Taylor's mouth, *The Times* exaggerated this to claim she struck at random, roaming Clavering with poisoned suckers 'which she slipped into the mouths of children at play.' They criticised Liberal politician William Ewart for his abolitionist stance on the death penalty, especially for poisoners who couldn't be left 'at large' because they would 'depopulate the neighbourhood', and couldn't be trusted in prison because 'they would poison their gaolers or their fellow-prisoners.' Quite how arsenic could be smuggled into a Victorian prison is left unexplained. They looked to 'the village surgeon and the druggist in the market town' to save them; the surgeon to assiduously report all suspicious illnesses to the authorities, and the druggist to take care who they sold poisons to: 'any measure which shall restrict or qualify the sale of arsenic will in the same degree put a check on the hideous crime.'

A household word in their mouths

While Sarah waited for her appointment with William Calcraft, the Sale of Arsenic Regulation Bill was being discussed in the House of Lords. Pressure from the public and the press had forced their hands, but looking at the Essex poison panic cases, it's not obvious how the regulation of arsenic's sale could have made much difference. It would have helped when trying to ascertain when and where Thomas Newport had bought arsenic, but as a farmer he had a legitimate use for it. Mary May had bought arsenic to poison rats and had not denied otherwise; in fact, the chemist who sold it said he knew Mary and had no reason not to sell it to her. Hannah Southgate clearly had some – witnesses had seen it in her house, being used somewhat carelessly – having her name in a register to say she had bought it would not have meant much. And it was known that Sarah Chesham had tried to buy arsenic and had been unable to. But *The Times* was waging its crusade against a terrifying 'system of poisoning' and the politicians bowed to their pressure.

The Bill was introduced by the Liberal George Howard, 7th Earl of Carlisle. Over the three readings of the Bill in March 1851, various correspondents had written to him to share their ideas, and eventually, on 24 March 1851 – the day before Sarah Chesham was to be executed – the Bill had its final reading in the Lords before being passed to the Commons. It was specifically arsenic that was to be restricted, not any other poison, because it was considered to be synonymous with 'poison' in parts of the country (such as Essex, one assumes, although the county and its cases are not specifically mentioned) where arsenic is spoken of lightly: 'a household word in their mouths'.

Its sale was to be restricted in such a way that those who needed arsenic legitimately would not be inconvenienced – free enterprise and individual liberty being sacred to Victorians – so a register would be kept by sellers of arsenic, the name of purchasers entered in it. They were to sign, and there was to be a witness. As arsenic was colourless, which added to its usefulness for underhand murders, they suggested it be coloured, either by indigo or soot, unless it was required for the arts or manufacturing. It was to be restricted just to male customers 'as several deplorable accidents had occurred from young children and female servants having been sent to purchase it.' The implication, of course, was that women were using it to kill. The philosopher John Stuart Mill strongly objected to this 'gross insult to every woman in the country' and wrote to the Home Secretary to tell him so:

> And for what reason, or under what incitement is this insult passed upon them? Because among the last dozen murders there were two or three cases, which attracted some public attention, of poisoning by women. Is it the part of a legislature to shape its laws to the accidental peculiarities of the latest crime reported in the newspapers? If the last two or three murderers had been men with red hair, as well might Parliament have rushed to pass an Act restricting all red-haired men from buying or possessing deadly weapons.

The comment about red-haired men may be Mill's barely veiled comment on the British Establishment's treatment of the Irish. The sale of arsenic worked on Mill's mind to the extent that part of his philosophical work *On Liberty* (1859) discussed how prevention of harm mitigates individual freedoms.

The Sale of Arsenic Regulation Act was finally passed on 5 June 1851, appearing much as it had in the Lords, although Mill would have been pleased to see that women were not barred from its purchase.

A fair or some holiday pleasure

Crowds began to gather outside Springfield Gaol before first light. It was Tuesday, 25 March 1851, and thousands had packed into Chelmsford by nine o'clock that morning, eager to catch a glimpse of a double hanging. Sarah Chesham had been found guilty and sentenced to death; so too had Thomas Drory. He had received far more attention in the press than Sarah, who, in the weeks leading up to execution, was begrudged the occasional line in reports that focused on Drory. He 'was bathed in tears' on his family's visits to him, and his confession attracted further fascination with his crime. The scene of Jael's murder was sought out by visitors and 'a tree growing near the spot has been stripped of its bark by its curiosity hunters in the "horrible" line.' The executions were 'the absorbing topic through the county, the interest increasing as the day fixed for their execution approaches.'

Some people were so keen to ensure a good spot for the execution that they had stayed in Chelmsford overnight, ensuring good business for local innkeepers. The crowd consisted mainly of the lower class, many of whom were women accompanied by their children. *The Times* waxed lyrical: 'smockfronted labourers, their highlows and gaiters spattered with mud, and their steps heavy with the number of miles they had travelled to "the hanging".' Some of the women 'had gay flowers in their bonnets, and evidently set up for rustic belles,' an uncanny echo of poor Jael Denny. Elderly matrons arrived with their families on 'domestic spring carts, pointing out to their young daughters how they could best see the execution.' There were a few farmers present, perhaps acquaintances of Drory and his family, or men who were intrigued by the execution of one of their number. Perhaps Thomas Newport was among them.

Despite 'several London thieves' taking the opportunity to pick pockets, stealing gold and silver watches from the crowd, 'a remarkable degree of order and decency, however, characterised the mob: there were no yells, hisses or groans.' Some of the spectators had travelled from the neighbouring counties of Suffolk and Cambridgeshire, and although some calculated that from 20,000 to 30,000 people attended, the more plausible estimate was still the vast number of some 10,000 to 12,000 people.

No petitions were circulated to save either Drory or Chesham from the gallows, the local papers considering this to be because the crimes were 'so atrocious and coldblooded' that 'the exertions of the most humane were paralysed.' It isn't clear why the Quakers did not speak out in this instance, although perhaps they felt with Mary May there was more chance of a reprieve, given that no woman had been executed at Chelmsford for so long: when Chesham came to the scaffold, Mary May had died in the same spot only three years before.

Just before nine o'clock, Drory and Chesham were brought onto the scaffold both in such a state of terror that they had to be supported by attendants. Sarah had to be lifted onto the drop, 'apparently in the most intense agony of mind, and every muscle of the body quivering in agitation.' Drory's lips moved silently, 'as if engaged in prayer.' *The Times*'s florid claim was that he had muttered, 'This is a faithful saying, and worthy of all acceptation, that Christ Jesus came into the world to save sinners – of whom I am the chief – of whom I am the chief,' although the prison governor later told the local papers that he had prayed in silence. Calcraft slipped caps over their heads and nooses around their necks, then disappeared from view to draw the bolt.

Some years earlier, the government had passed a law that no one beside prison employees were allowed at executions, so the governor of Springfield Gaol had rejected requests from 'several gentlemen' who had wanted to be present or to see the bodies afterwards – a phrenologist had asked if he could take casts of their heads. Press reporters were not allowed in either, so newspapers had to print a statement given by the governor, although their reporters could be in the crowd with the thronging mass of gaiter–clad labourers and country belles.

No one could agree how long it took Drory and Chesham to die: the *Essex Standard* said Drory died with 'but one convulsive shake' and Sarah had 'struggled considerably for two or three minutes.' The *Chelmsford Chronicle* said 'both culprits died hard, the struggles of both visible for many minutes,' and *The Times* had it that Drory took four or five minutes, and Sarah six or seven.

After an hour, their bodies were cut down. As part of the sentence for murder, Drory's remains were buried within the grounds of Springfield Gaol, as had Mary May's been; Sarah Chesham's sentence made no such specification, so her son, Philip, loaded his mother's body into a cart, and drove it back to Clavering.

A man called John Copland wrote 'a well-timed and touching little paper' called 'The Condemned Ones', and circulated 3,000 copies of it among the crowd. It was reproduced in full by the *Essex Standard*, urging those attending the executions to view it as a moral lesson, rather than an excuse for a party.

His tract had to compete with the more lurid productions of the ballad and broadside sellers, who circulated among the crowd as soon as the bodies of the condemned had finished twitching on their ropes. Several versions were printed for Thomas Drory's crime, the ballad sellers capitalising on the crime that had seized the public attention. A ballad seller interviewed by Henry Mayhew said, 'We worked it every way. Drory had every chance given to him. We had half-sheets, and copies of verses, and books.' The murder was even subject of an engraving that was for sale on London streets and possibly at the execution, reproduced by Mayhew as an example of the form. Titled 'The Horrible and Bar-bari-ous Murder' of Jael Denny, there is something uncomfortably sexual about the image, showing the victim prostrate on the ground as Thomas sits on her flourishing the ends of the rope he has tied about her neck. The hyphenated and misspelt 'barbarous' suggests the education of the artwork's target customers.

Sarah Chesham's execution generated a jolly ditty flung together by Hodges of Seven Dials in London:

> *Behold a wretched woman,*
> *The mother of a family,*
> *For the murder of her husband,*
> *Doomed to die upon a tree.*

As is typical of these productions, they are full of assumptions parading as facts:

> *On the twenty-eighth of May,*
> *The wretched woman she did go,*
> *To a shop to buy the fatal poison,*
> *That was proved her overthrow.*

EXECUTION OF SARAH CHESHAM.

For the MURDER of RICHARD CHESHAM, her Husband, by Poison.

Air.—"The Waggon Train."

BEHOLD a wretched married woman,
The mother of a family,
For the murder of her husband,
Doomed to die upon a tree;
Oh! whatever could possess you,
On that sad and fatal day,
For to prepare the dreadful poison
And take her husband's life away.

CHORUS.

See a wretched wife and mother,
Borne down by grief and misery,
Because she did her husband murder,
Doomed to die upon a tree.

Sarah Chesham is the wretched culprit,
At Clavering, near Newport she did dwell,
Her husband was an honest labourer,
Respected and esteemed full well.
A husband kind—a tender father,
He was unto his family,
Besides he was an upright member
Of a Burial Society.

On the twenty-eighth of May,
The wretched woman she did go
To a shop to buy the fatal poison,
Which has proved her overthrow;
The dreadful dose she gave her husband,
Soon after which Richard Chesham died,
And she when taxed with the foul murder,
Strongly the deed denied.

At length suspicion fell upon her,
And to justice she was brought,
That no one would the crime discover,
The sad and wretched murderess thought,
She slew the partner of her bosom,
It was we read for cruel gain,

And made her darling children suffer,
Distressed and overcome with pain.

For a paltry sum of money,
She did her lawful husband slay,
And for no other cause but lucre,
Did she take his life away,
The judge on her pronounced the sentence,
Sarah Chesham you must hanged be,
At the front of Chelmsford Jail,
On the dismal fatal tree.

When she was at the holy altar,
She did a solemn vow then give,
Her husband dear to love and cherish,
Whilst God permitted her to live;
But she the solemn vow has broken,
Wicked, base, deceitful wife,
Barbarous and cruel mother,
Doomed to die in prime of life.

The solemn knell for her is tolling,
Numbers flock her end to see,
A cruel wife, a wretched mother,
To approach the fatal tree.
From whence her frame when life is ended,
Will in disgrace be borne away,
And placed within Chelmsford Jail,
To lie unto the judgment day.

Male and females, take a warning,
By Sarah Chesham's dreadful fate,
Ponder well, night, noon, and morning,
Before, alas! it is too late.
Let not even Satan tempt you,
To desert from virtue's way,
And think upon that wretched woman,
Who did for gain her husband slay.

Hodges, Printer, Wholesale Toy Warehouse,
31, Dudley Street, 7 Dials.

Execution of Sarah Chesham. Broadside ballad.

But there was no evidence she had bought arsenic, and certainly no specific date put forward to suggest when she had. Confusing Sarah Chesham with Mary May, the ballad claims she killed her husband '*For a paltry sum of money*' and then she would be buried '*within Chelmsford Jail, To lie unto the Judgment Day*', which wasn't correct either.

Although the crowds had been quiet leading up to the execution, when they broke up afterwards, it was remarked that their conduct was light, and throughout the day Chelmsford was like a fair or a holiday, 'and at various public houses scenes of sickening riot, noisy brawls, and fights took place, as was to be expected from the congregating together of such a multitude of low and vicious characters.'

The Times reported on the executions the following day, wrongly naming the last woman hanged in Chelmsford as 'Anne May'. 'Mrs Chesham was said to have been intimate with her; but she denied this stoutly, and they appear to have lived in totally different parts of the county.' It was *The Times* itself that had claimed they were acquainted, and only now, once both women were dead, did they suggest they might have been wrong. They said Sarah Chesham had been tried twice before, as if at separate assizes, and had been saved on one occasion by 'the scruples of a Quaker opposed to capital punishment', incorrectly referring to the petition got up by the Chelmsford Quakers for Mary May. They took pleasure in Drory's written statement of guilt, which was 'evidently the composition of a very illiterate person' and 'it throws a curious light upon the amount of education which Drory possessed.' Shades, perhaps, of their view back in 1846 that Essex was 'an uneducated county'.

Their leading article, published the same day, steers a strange middle way between the pro- and abolition camps. It expresses horror and disgust at 'the hideous spectacle of a judicial slaughter' but defends capital punishment as long as people continue to commit murder.

The executions were reported across the country, in typical style, emphasising the undeniable guilt of the condemned and the horror of their crimes. The *Royal Cornwall Gazette* said what the local Essex papers had skirted around: Sarah was 'an awful example of those of her sex, who, in the county of Essex more especially have been guilty of the frightful crime of arsenical poisoning, for the purpose of obtaining paltry allowances from burial clubs'. Perhaps this confusion for onlookers between Mary May and

Sarah Chesham was caused by the fact that no concrete motive had been put forward for Sarah to have murdered her husband. Cornwall has always had problems with arsenic occurring naturally in its water sources, due to its mineral make-up; it had no need for home-grown poisoners.

Home again, home again, jiggity-jig

When Philip Chesham arrived home with the corpse of his infamous mother in his cart, her coffin was opened 'and the curiosity of many was allowed to be gratified.' It is possible this was when a phrenologist examined her head, having been prevented from doing so at the prison. He claimed, based on his somewhat dubious specialism, that he had never seen 'Destructiveness' more developed in any skull.

Sarah had been executed on the Tuesday; on Friday, 28 March 1851, her mortal remains were laid to rest in Clavering churchyard. No religious service was performed, and 'there were a great many spectators, who generally preserved a becoming order and decency during the ceremony.'

But the *Sunday Times* – only allied to *The Times* because it chose to give itself a similar name, implying a connection that did not exist – printed a penny-a-liner story that the local Essex newspapers quietly mocked. They said Sarah Chesham was buried in 'Wix, near Clavering', demonstrating once

Clavering parish church.

again the shaky understanding those outside Essex had of its geography, the two villages being nearly 60 miles apart. She had been laid in a temporary grave, as her relatives hoped she might eventually be allowed a Christian burial, but 'to their surprise the grave has been opened, and the coffin and body have been carried off. The whole case is shrouded in mystery, and has caused much excitement.' The *Essex Standard* said it was a 'communication which we by no means vouch for the truth of', and it does seem unlikely.

Sarah's name was entered in Clavering's burial register by Reverend George Brookes, who had given evidence at her original trials in support of her good character. Instead of writing down her abode, he wrote 'Executed at Chelmsford 25th March' and then added 'No service'. Two days before Sarah's burial, Susan Newport, Thomas's mother, had been laid to rest in the same churchyard.

The day after Sarah's burial, Thomas Newport's brother, William, attended the magistrates' sitting. Thomas was complaining that he had attended the assize in Chelmsford from Monday to Friday, but wasn't called to give evidence, and hadn't been allowed his expenses, unlike the other witnesses. The magistrates' clerk said he had applied in the usual way after the trial for the witnesses' expenses, but Mr Straight, the clerk of the arraigns, decided 'that Mr T. Newport's were not allowed.' The magistrates told William that his brother would have to enquire of Mr Straight himself 'the reason for withholding his allowance'. He does not appear to have pursued it: it was, perhaps, one way the county could punish him.

We see a snapshot of the people of Clavering immediately after Sarah's execution, as the 1851 census was taken on the night of 30 March. To the west of the village, Thomas Newport was living with his widowed father at Curls Manor Farm.

In a cottage on Water Lane, James Parker, Sarah's father, is listed as the head of household, living with Sarah's three surviving sons: Philip, John, and George, the youngest of the Cheshams, aged eleven. All three were working as agricultural labourers. In addition, there was another Chesham orphan, Harriet, with her husband, Nathan Chipperfield. Then two visitors – George and Susan Chipperfield, presumably Nathan's brother and his wife.

Over on the next page of the census book were the Cheshams' near-neighbours: Hannah Phillips with the husband she may or may not have wanted to kill.

Chapter 5

'I alone suspected her'

Across the other side of Essex that same night in 1851, Robert May was living in a cottage in Wix with his 15-year-old stepson, William Everett. The motherless Jemima, only surviving daughter of Robert and Mary May, was living with her aunt and uncle, William and Martha May; she was five years old.

Susannah Forster, who had taken Mary May that fateful day to Harwich to sign up Spratty Watts in the burial club, lived alone. She was thirty-one, her occupation given as 'Governess of National School and Post Office'. The household immediately after hers in the census schedule is that of the Reverend George Wilkins, who had aided Inspector Raison in his investigation of Mary May.

Wilkins had not kept out of the newspapers. At the end of 1849, the year after Mary May's trial and execution, he horrified many by his behaviour at the Ardleigh Farmers' Club dinner. After competitions for ploughing and cottage garden produce, they retired for dinner at The King's Head inn. Reports of these agricultural meetings, attended by farmers and vicars, often appear in local newspapers, reading as boozy occasions with cheering and 'hear, hear' punctuating reports of people's speeches, even though they open with a toast to the clergy and Queen Victoria. Wilkins, who enjoyed involving himself in the business of rural life, made a toast to fox hunting, saying that 'if they had more amusement and less preaching they should be a much happier and more moral people.' It is unlikely he was being entirely serious, merely joining in with the tipsy banter. But there were complaints. The *London Record* copied the *Essex Standard*'s report, and someone signing themselves 'A Protestant' wrote a letter larded with quotes from Scripture to the *Essex Standard*'s editor. They printed the letter and in the same edition worked up an editorial condemning the vicar for what he had said, which they hadn't passed comment on the week before when they originally printed it.

Another view of Wix parish church.

A letter from Wilkins was published in the *Essex Standard* on 21 December 1849, but rather than explain his misguided joke at the farmers' dinner, instead he addressed a more serious incident in which he had been involved: the trial of Mary May. It would appear that Wilkins had been receiving poison pen letters from several 'anonymous correspondents, who, with hearts teeming with malice, pretend to pray for my soul, charitably charge me with causing the murder of Spratty Watts by Mary May, and also of many other murders and other deep crimes'.

It isn't clear whether this had come about by his recent publicised gaff, or had been going on ever since the death of Spratty Watts, aka William Constable, sent by locals or the sort of people who would later write to the papers during Jack the Ripper's reign of terror. In his letter, Wilkins explained Mary's family background, that she was not a native of Wix but in early life had lived in nearby Great Oakley, and that she had come to Wix from Ramsey after her first husband's death to live with Robert May. He implies they were cohabiting, and said they did so only because they couldn't afford to marry, hence he had paid the fee for them. He wrote that he was already suspicious of Mary, and as soon as he heard of Spratty's death, suspected at once that he'd been poisoned. He then unearthed the motive – that Spratty was in a burial club – and informed the coroner. He offered to pay for Mary May's defence counsel, even though he was convinced of her guilt, but Serjeant Jones, who had financial worries of his own at the time, and Chambers, refused to accept his money. Wilkins said that it was only right that these facts were known, and he hoped they would 'strike with shame – if they know what shame is – those anonymous and canting hypocrites who represent the Minister of Wix to be a murderer.'

It is no wonder Hannah Southgate had moved away and changed her name as soon as she could; not long after Sarah Chesham's execution, the Mays and Reverend Wilkins would find themselves in the press again.

On the last meeting of Robert and his wife before her execution, Mary threatened, in jest according to the newspapers, that she would haunt him if he married again. Indeed, she did haunt him, when in 1851 her name appeared in the papers once more, in the press coverage of Sarah Chesham's trial. Whether he believed his late wife to have been guilty or not, Robert could not escape her infamy, but he was making an attempt to move on.

In June 1851, he posted banns in Wix church, intending to marry Susannah Forster; she was pregnant by him. But Robert was troubled. He had often mentioned to Martha, his sister-in-law, and Caroline, his niece, Mary's threat to haunt him, and Martha said he was 'weak-minded from his birth', a man whose mood was often very low. He was frequently silent, in thought, as was observed by his family as well as fellow agricultural labourers out in the field. William Lungley, with whom he worked, said that, just before posting the banns, he had gone for an hour without speaking, and hoed very fast, some distance away from them.

On the evening of Sunday, 8 June, Robert had been to see William and Martha, and on his way home saw Susannah for all of five minutes. According to Martha, he lived entirely alone, so it is possible that William Everett had moved out from his stepfather's cottage in the lead up to his marriage. Martha helped Robert with his housekeeping; arriving as usual at his cottage at 7.20 am the next morning to make his bed, the door was locked. There was no answer when she called, so she got up to the bedroom window, but could not see him inside and assumed he had gone to work.

Martha's 15-year-old daughter, Caroline, managed to climb in through the bedroom window, and when she got to the staircase, she found Robert dead. He had hanged himself.

An inquest was opened the next day by William Codd, finding himself once again in Wix. The *Essex Standard*, in their report, reminded readers of Mary May's crime, and that it was 'the first of the series of suspected poisonings in that locality, the investigation of which excited so much sensation in the public mind'. They commented that the cottage where Robert had committed suicide was the same one in which William Constable had been murdered, and reported that Wix's locals hoped it would be demolished as 'it is inferior to many pig-styes and its existence only serves to keep alive a morbid feeling from the horrid crimes of which it has been the theatre.' The *Chelmsford Chronicle* went further and called it a hovel that 'represents an almost unparalleled exhibition of wretchedness.' Despite being the village schoolmistress, they noticed that Susannah Forster 'made her mark instead of signing her depositions.' The jury returned a verdict of 'Temporary Mental Derangement' and Robert was buried by Reverend Wilkins on 12 May. For posterity, he added a note:

Robert May hanged himself. He was the husband of Mary May who was hanged at Chelmsford for the murder of Wm Constable which she effected by administering arsenic in some porter on or about June 8 1848. He hung himself June 8 1851.

It was only Reverend Wilkins, so keenly involved in the tragic events in his parish, who pointed out this coincidence with the dates. On 17 July 1851, he baptised William, Susannah Forster's illegitimate child, and less than a week later buried the little boy.

A week after the inquest into Robert's death, another letter by Reverend Wilkins was published by the *Essex Standard*, correcting them on their report that stated that Susannah had, by false representation to the Harwich burial club, aided Mary May in her crime. Wilkins claimed that when he and Inspector Raison made their investigations, they discovered that she 'had nothing to do in the matter' and had given 'no character of the man, nor was any one asked for or required.' He blamed instead the eagerness of the burial club to increase their membership. He expressed concern that this error would do serious damage to Wix's school. But the editor wrote a response in the paper, referring back to the columns it had filled in 1848, and pointed out that Wilkins was wrong.

In their next issue, the *Essex Standard* printed another letter by the meddlesome vicar where he explained that he had not intended his previous letter for publication; it presumably had caused him some embarrassment. He said that at the time Mary May entered her brother in the burial club 'there was no imputation on her character' and, like an ecclesiastical Poirot, he claimed, 'No one except myself believed that she was capable of committing such a crime; I alone suspected her, and by a seeming interference of Providence made the discovery.'

This time the editor didn't respond.

Wilkins appeared in the newspapers again in 1856, when he had to be investigated by the diocesan bishop at Colchester Castle. It caused a stir, being reported in newspapers as far away as Wiltshire. On 4 May, the day of public thanksgiving for the end of the Crimean War, Wilkins broke off during the reading 'and began an address to the congregation, commenting upon what he considered had been the immoral conduct of one of his parishioners.' This man was James Eagle, a farmer at Park Hall in Wix, who rose from his pew 'and in profane language accused Mr Wilkins of falsehood.' The vicar 'rejoined in the most coarse and vehement manner; and an altercation ensued between them of a character which would disgrace the lowest public house.' The service ended early; the parishioners poured out of the church, disgusted by what they had witnessed. As punishment, James Eagle was forced to donate £20 to the Colchester and Essex Hospital. Wilkins was given a severe reprimand by the bishop, who acknowledged there were people in Wix 'who entertain malicious feelings towards you – very unjustly, as I have reason to believe.'

Perhaps Wilkins was never able to escape the ill feeling of those who thought he had acted inappropriately in the case of Mary May; even so, he continued as the reverend incumbent of Wix until his death in 1877, at the age of ninety. He earnt himself an affectionate obituary in the newspaper with which he had been so enthusiastic a correspondent.

Inspector Samuel Raison, who had been so diligent in his investigation of alleged poisoning in the Tendring Hundred, did not have so long a career. In December 1850, Raison was one of several policemen called to attend a suspicious fire in Manningtree, at the property of hairdresser and toy dealer George Cauch Viall. The day before Raison was to give evidence at the inquest into the suspected arson, he fell ill with paralysis. He recovered slightly and insisted that he should give evidence, so he was taken to Manningtree in a close conveyance. He did not recover sufficiently to work, but luckily he had entered himself in a benevolent club, which would support him while he was incapacitated.

Unfortunately, the club's rules specified that if a member travelled a mile from their home while claiming sickness, they would be ejected from the club and receive no money. It is ironic that Raison, who had been so assiduous in investigating the burial clubs in his local area, should come to grief with the benevolent club he had joined himself. Raison, as a respected member of his community, had friends in high places. Two gentleman arrived, unimpressed, at the pub where the club met. 'The beer can was constantly being handed round, and it seemed as if it was necessary to the discharge of club duties that a certain quantity of beer should be consumed.' The club's committee tried to fob them off, saying, 'Ah! If it had not been a policeman there would not have been this noise about it.' This is probably true, but Raison's supporters managed to reinstate him in the club.

By 1861, Raison's occupation on the census is 'Invalid, former policeman' – it seems his health never fully recovered, and he died in 1868, at the age of fifty-four.

Susannah Forster, after the tragic loss of her fiancé and child in such a short space of time, continued to work as a schoolmistress. By 1861 she had moved back to her hometown of Harwich; perhaps she needed to evade Wix's wagging tongues. She lived alone until her death in 1881.

Tracing the sons of Mary May has proved impossible. However, Mary's daughter Jemima May became a domestic servant and by 1881 she was working in Banstead in Surrey – ironically, a place that appeared in the life of another woman caught up in the poison panic. It seems that Jemima, who would only have had vague memories of her parents, never returned to the county of her birth.

The Cheshams

Not long after his mother's execution, Philip Chesham was found guilty at the 1851 Summer Assize of stealing a waistcoat. This small crime, for which he was sentenced to six months' hard labour, earned him far more column inches than it warranted, due to newspapers across the country being eager to make the connection between him and his mother, 'the notorious Essex poisoner'. He continued to live in Clavering for some time, where he married and raised a family, but by 1901 he was in Saffron Walden Workhouse. He was perhaps unable to work due to old age, and he died in 1902, in his seventies. His brother John Chesham had died in 1855, aged twenty-two; this was one death, at least, that no one could accuse his mother of.

The following year, their sister Harriet and her husband Nathan Chipperfield emigrated to Australia, taking Harriet's youngest brother George with them. Like many, they would have seen Australia as an opportunity to escape the hard grind of life as a British agricultural labourer, but it's likely they may also have wished to escape a village where their family had such infamous connections. Sadly, George, then aged seventeen, died almost as soon as they landed in Sydney.

Hannah Phillips, whose testimony had been so instrumental in Sarah Chesham's ultimate downfall, died in 1859. Her husband remarried in 1860; his second wife, Mary, was, by some strange twist of fate, the widow of Sarah Chesham's brother, John Parker.

Thomas Newport moved away from Clavering and settled with his wife at Pledgdon Hall in Henham. He raised a large family and was a wealthy farmer and maltster – in 1871 he farmed nearly 400 acres. He died in 1892, aged seventy-four.

Lydia Taylor, who it could be argued set the Essex poison panic in motion, married in 1847. She and her husband had several children, and they continued to live in Manuden until the 1860s, when they moved to Cheshunt in Hertfordshire. This is where Lydia died in 1873, aged forty-seven.

Sarah Chesham did not vanish from local memory. Whenever murder was done in Clavering, her name was mentioned in the press. In 1862, Samuel Law and his baby were murdered by his wife, Rebecca. They lived at Starling's Green in Clavering, 'a lonely situation, apparently suited for such a deed of blood, and the parish is already notorious for the dreadful child poisonings which were perpetrated there a few years ago.' Even though Sarah had been acquitted at the time, her later trial was effectively for those earlier deaths too, and she had entered history as a serial killer. Rebecca Law was acquitted at trial, it being medical opinion that she was a lunatic.

In 1903, the body of Camille Cecile Holland was found in the grounds of Moat Farm in Clavering. She had disappeared four years earlier, murdered by her partner. There was great interest in the case, sightseers visiting Clavering where they could buy postcards of the farm; 'oranges and nuts were sold as at a village fair.' The *Chelmsford Chronicle* took this opportunity to dust off its back issues and remind their readers of Sarah Chesham; Camille's murder was 'not the first sensational mystery which has been furnished by the parish of Clavering.'

The *Chelmsford Chronicle*, in 1908, ran an interview with an 89-year-old former policeman about his memories of Essex. He had been in the crowd when Mary May, Sarah Chesham, Thomas Drory and, in 1853, Charles Saunders, another murderer, were executed. Twenty years later, they interviewed Elizabeth Hasler, aged 102. 'She has a wonderful memory,' the

Another view of Clavering parish church.

paper commented, even though she recalled seeing the execution of Sarah Chesham, who had, Elizabeth misremembered, 'poisoned four husbands.' It was her sister's 'young man' who had taken them on this delightful family day out; it's tempting to wonder if Elizabeth, who would have been twenty-five at the time, had been one of the 'rustic belles' with flower-trimmed bonnets remarked on by *The Times*. That same year, a fire in Clavering claimed a house in the village, which the *Chelmsford Chronicle* incorrectly claimed 'to have been inhabited, years ago, by a doctor who supplied a woman there with arsenic which she used to poison her husband.' Sarah Chesham had passed into legend.

The fate of a convict

The afterlife of Emma Elizabeth Hume, transported for life for the attempted poisoning of her husband, is worth a brief digression. Unlike the Chipperfields, who had travelled to Australia by assisted passage, Emma had set sail in chains. Her husband, who was much older than her, died before her ship had even left port, so she arrived in Australia as a widow at the age of twenty-four.

Almost as soon as Emma arrived in Tasmania in 1849, she applied for a marriage permission, but it was deferred, so she tried again in 1850, this time choosing a different potential husband; her request was accepted. She was given a conditional pardon in 1857, but in 1859, she was in trouble with the law once more when she stole some boots and other wearing apparel. After the death of her second husband, she married again in 1876, and died herself five years later.

Lucky Hannah Southgate?

Neither hanged nor transported, Hannah Southgate changed her surname to Welham and lived in London with her husband. Her former servant, Phoebe Read, died at the end of 1851. By 1861, John and Hannah were tobacconists on St George's Street in Tower Hamlets. John appears on the census both with Hannah and also as John Southgate, in his parents' house in Wix; it's possible he was visiting to collect rents on his properties. In July of the same year, Hannah's daughter Emily Lavinia Ham married Michael Hall, a plasterer from Bethnal Green; they went on to have eight children.

John and Hannah ran their tobacconist's shop at the same location, under their assumed surname, until John's death in 1884, aged sixty-nine. He had been in Wix on business and was found dead in his bed. His death was sudden, so there was an inquest and the post-mortem found that he had died of heart disease. He had written his will in 1866, under the name John Southgate, leaving everything to Hannah, and in 1885 an auction was held at the Waggon pub in Wix to sell his property.

What would Hannah do, now that 'her Johnny' was dead, the man who many thought she had killed for to be with? In February 1886 Hannah Welham was admitted to Banstead Asylum. She was sixty-seven, suffering from senile dementia with an impaired memory. Studies have shown that dementia can be brought on by stressful events in early middle age, and it is possible that living in daily fear of her past being discovered had caused her mental faculties to give way.

But even from behind the walls of a lunatic asylum, Hannah managed to appear once more in the press. The past sometimes appears to dementia patients more clearly than the present, and this might be what prompted Hannah to challenge her incarceration in Banstead Asylum. She claimed that her legal settlement was Wix, which would mean Hannah being moved to an asylum in Essex. The Tendring Union objected to this, saying that for many years her husband had paid his rates in St George in the East, therefore it was the place of her settlement, according to the Poor Law. No sensible replies could be gained from Hannah; the decayed state of her memory caused her to claim that she had been married three times. Her request was declined and she remained in Banstead.

On her admission to the asylum, she had been a quiet patient, but as time passed she 'gradually became quite lost' with 'faulty habits'. She got very impulsive but became more and more feeble. It was Hannah's heart that killed her, rather than Calcraft's noose, on 12 December 1907. She was eighty-eight years old.

She had been born at the end of the reign of George III, and watched from the window of her East End tobacconist's shop as London's population swelled by millions. She survived cholera epidemics, and would have seen

Jeff Bewsey, a descendant of Hannah Southgate's daughter, Emily Lavinia Ham, shown here with an old Jamaican fire engine.

The Great Exhibition, the limping soldiers that came home from Crimea, the coming of the underground trains. The Royal Albert Hall was opened, and Cleopatra's Needle was erected. There were more women accused of poisoning: Ellen Kittel, Mary Ann Cotton, Florence Maybrick. Hannah was admitted to Banstead in the same year that the first Sherlock Holmes story was published; two years later, Whitechapel, near her East End home, became the feared site of another murder panic. This time the weapon was not a tasteless, colourless powder allegedly administered by loved ones, but a slashing blade wielded by a dangerous stranger.

It has been possible to trace Jeff Bewsey, one of Hannah's great-great-great-grandsons, now a retired London firefighter. I asked Jeff if there were any family stories about Hannah, but he confessed that he had known nothing at all about her – no one in the family had mentioned her. He is, however, pleased to find out his claim to fame; his ancestor's infamous association with the Essex poison panic. Emily Lavinia's family had perhaps hoped that with the passing of the years, the memory of Hannah would fade and eventually disappear. But the past is always with us, like a muffled voice on the other side of a wall that sometimes grows distinct enough to hear.

Timeline

1845

January   Joseph and James Chesham die in Clavering.

1846

August   Sarah Chesham arrested for poisoning Solomon Taylor; inquest opens into deaths of her sons, Joseph and James Chesham.

November   *Lucretia*, by Edward Bulwer-Lytton, published.

1847

March   Sarah Chesham on trial for murders of Solomon Taylor, and Joseph and James Chesham. Acquitted.

April   Catherine Foster executed in Bury St Edmunds for the murder of her husband with arsenic.

April   Thomas Ham dies in Tendring.

July   Emma Elizabeth Hume convicted at Chelmsford of attempted murder of her husband with sugar of lead.

July   John Southgate marries Hannah, widow of Thomas Ham, in Tendring.

1848

June   Death of William Constable, aka Spratty Watts, in Wix. Inquest opens.

July   Mary May convicted at Chelmsford of the murder of William Constable, aka Spratty Watts.

August   Mary May executed at Chelmsford.

August   Inquest opens into the death of Thomas Ham in Tendring.

September   Inquest opens into the death of Nathaniel Button in Ramsey.

1849

March	Hannah Southgate on trial for murder of Thomas Ham, her husband. Acquitted.
August	Mary Anne Geering convicted of murder, poisoning several family members with arsenic.
Summer– Autumn	Cholera epidemic across Britain.
October	Trial of Frederick George Manning and Maria Manning at the Old Bailey, for the murder of Patrick O'Connor. Both executed the following month.

1850

April	William Ballantine defending prisoner accused of defrauding the Southgates, at the Old Bailey.
May	Richard Chesham dies in Clavering; inquest opens into his death.
September	Sarah Chesham arrested.
October	Murder of Jael Denny in Doddinghurst.

1851

March	Sarah Chesham convicted of attempted murder of her husband, Richard Chesham, with arsenic.
March	Thomas Drory convicted of murdering his lover, Jael Denny.
March	Chesham and Drory executed at Chelmsford.
June	Suicide of Robert May, widower of Mary May.
June	Sale of Arsenic Regulation Act passed.

Acknowledgements

Firstly I would like to thank you, dear reader, for choosing this book: I hope you enjoyed it. Many thanks to Linne Matthews, my lovely editor, and to Pen & Sword for commissioning this book. Slightly embarrassed thanks must go to all my family and friends who have had their ear bent about poisons, Victorians, burial clubs, assizes, etc. etc. etc. in the past year; I apologise if you were put off your dinner.

Thank you to my Mum and my brother Peter for driving me around Essex, and for my little brother Duncan who came with us (and accidentally ended up in the photo of Wix church). Thanks to my friend Charlotte for our trip to Colchester on the bus (who also ended up in a photo by accident). Thanks to Dad and Sharon for their unfailing enthusiasm. Thanks to Gordon Wallace, Cindy Lilley, Angela Grayston and Jeff Bewsey for the photos. Thanks to Verity for the arsenic bottles, and Olivia for the gin. Thank you to the Birmingham chapter of the Romance Novelists' Association for their encouragement (I'm sure there's a novel in this somewhere) and to the helpful Australian genealogists who pieced together the afterlife of Emma Elizabeth Hume. A big shout out to Julie and her daughter at The Fox and Hounds in Clavering, who do a marvellous lunch; to the chap behind the bar of The Waggon in Wix for knowing who Mary May was; and to the landlord of The Castle inn in Ramsey who showed me the site of the Nelson's Head inn and told me about the 1979 Ramsey Siege (he does a marvellous lunch, too).

Thanks also to the Essex Record Office, the Essex Police Museum, The National Archives, London Metropolitan Archives, the US National Library of Medicine, the British Library, and Library Services and the Cadbury Research Library at the University of Birmingham.

Phew. I think that's everyone.

Further Reading

Others have written about Sarah Chesham, Mary May and Hannah Southgate before. Judith Flanders includes them as part of her encyclopaedic study of the Victorian fondness for murder in *The Invention of Murder*; if you want more nineteenth-century crime then you can do no worse than start with her. When I started to research the Essex poison panic beyond newspapers and parish registers, I found Victoria Nagy's article about Mary May and burial clubs very enlightening. She has since written a scholarly monograph on the cases of Chesham, May and Southgate, but it went to press just as I started to write *Poison Panic*, so I am yet to read it. Don Budds, a Tendring Hundred local historian (and distant cousin of mine) writes about May and Southgate in his pamphlet 'Arsenic & Old Wix' – he and I have drawn similar conclusions from the parish registers. Jill Louise Ainsley's MA thesis, *The Ordeal of Sarah Chesham*, based mainly on contemporary newspapers, ably takes to task previous writers who have read *The Times*'s sensationalist leaders at face value.

As I am writing from a genealogical angle, and as an Essex woman with personal ties to some of the cases, I hope my approach will add a new voice to the body of work that already exists on this subject.

Bibliography

Alpert, Michael, *London 1849: A Victorian Murder Story*, Pearson, Harlow, 2004.

Ballantine, Serjeant (William), *Some Experiences of a Barrister's Life*, 8th ed., Richard Bentley, London, 1883.

Barker, Hannah, *Newspapers, politics and English society, 1695–1855*, Pearson, Harlow, 2000.

Borowitz, Albert, *The Bermondsey Horror*, Robson Books, London, 1988.

Bowley, A.L., 'The Statistics of Wages in the United Kingdom During the Last Hundred Years, part 1', *Journal of the Royal Statistical Society*, Vol 61(4), 1898, p. 704.

Bronte, Emily, *Wuthering Heights*, Puffin (Penguin), London, 1994 (first published 1847).

Brown, Lucy, *Victorian news and newspapers*, Clarendon Press, Oxford, 1985.

Bulwer-Lytton, Edward, *A Word to the Public*, Tauchnitz, Leipzig, 1847.

Census of Great Britain, 1841, *Abstract of the answers and returns made pursuant to acts 3 & 4 Vic. c.99 and 4 Vic. c.7 intituled respectively 'An act for taking an account of the population of Great Britain', and 'An act to amend the acts of the last session for taking an account of the population'*, Enumeration Abstract, BPP 1843 XXII, Home Office, London, 1843.

Chadwick, Edwin, *Report on the sanitary condition of the labouring population of Great Britain : a supplementary report on the results of a special inquiry into the practice of interment in towns made at the request of Her Majesty's Principal Secretary of State for the Home Department*, W. Clowes, London, 1843.

Dasent, Arthur Irwin, *John Thadeus Delane, editor of The Times. His Life & Correspondence*, Vol. 1, John Murray, London, 1908.

Daunton, Martin, 'Society and economic life' in Matthew, Colin, ed., *The Nineteenth Century. The British Isles: 1815-1901*, Oxford University Press, 2000.

Dickens, Charles, *Hard Times*, first published 1854.

Developing Treatments: Poisons as Treatments, Museum of the Royal Pharmaceutical Society, London, 2006. Retrieved from www.rpharms.com/museum.

Emsley, Clive, *The English Police: a political and social history*, 2nd ed., Longman, London, 1996.

Emsley, John, *Elements of Murder: A History of Poison*, Oxford University Press, 2005.

Flanders, Judith, *The Invention of Murder: How the Victorians Revelled in Death and Detection and Created Modern Crime*, HarperPress, London, 2011.

Gaskill, Malcolm, *Witchfinders: A Seventeenth-Century English Tragedy*, John Murray, London, 2006.

Hardy, Sheila, *Arsenic in the Dumplings: A Casebook of Historic Poisonings in Suffolk*, History Press, Stroud, 2010.

Hurren, Elizabeth, 'Patients' rights: from Alder Hey to the Nuremberg Code', 6th May 2002, in *History & Policy*, Retrieved 6 June 2015, www.historyandpolicy.org.

Johansson, L. et al, 'Common psychosocial stressors in middle-aged women related to longstanding distress and increased risk of Alzheimer's disease: a 38-year longitudinal population study', *BMJ Open*, 2013.

Johnson, Steven., *The Ghost Map: A street, a city, an epidemic and the hidden power of urban networks*, Penguin, London, 2008.

Lewis, J.R., *The Victorian Bar*, Robert Hale, London, 1982.

Mayhew, Henry, *London Labour and the London Poor*, Vol. 1: The London Street Folk, *Morning Chronicle*, London, 1851.

Mill, John Stuart, *The Collected Works of John Stuart Mill, Volume XIV: The Later Letters of John Stuart Mill, 1849–1873 part I*. Eds. www.oll.libertyfund.org.

Nagy, Victoria M., 'Narratives in the courtroom: Female poisoners in mid-nineteenth-century England', *European Journal of Criminology*, 2014. Vol. 11(2), pp. 213–27.

Napp, Andrew & Baldwin, William, *The Newgate Calendar*, Vol. 4, London, (year unknown).

Old Bailey Proceedings Online (www.oldbaileyonline.org, version 7.2, 05 July 2015), April 1850, trial of JOHN SADLER (t18500408-694) and May 1850, trial of JOHN SADLER (t18500506-990).

Parry, Leonard A., ed., *Trial of Dr Smethurst (Notable British Trials)*, William Hodge, Edinburgh & London, 1931.

Peacock, A.J., 'Village radicalism in East Anglia, 1800–1850', in *Rural discontent in nineteenth-century Britain* by J.P.D. Dunbabin, Faber & Faber, London, 1974.

Phegley, Jennifer, *Courtship and Marriage in Victorian England*, Praeger, Santa Barbara, 2012.

Probert, Rebecca, *Marriage Law for Genealogists: The Definitive Guide*, Takeaway, Kenilworth, 2012.

Rai, S. and Thomas, W.M., 'Diagnosis of abdominal tuberculosis: the importance of laparoscopy', in *J R Soc Med*. 2003 Dec; 96(12): 586–8.

Robb, George, 'Circe in crinoline: domestic poisonings in Victorian England', *Journal of Family History*, 22(2), April 1997, pp. 176–7.

Rowley, Sheila V., *Little Baddow: The history of an Essex village, part three*, Little Baddow, 1979, retrieved from: www.mel-thompson.co.uk.

Storey, Neil R., *A Grim Almanac of Essex*, History Press, Stroud, 2013.

Summerscale, Kate, *The Suspicions of Mr Whicher: or The Murder at Road Hill House*. Bloomsbury, London, 2008.

Taylor, Alfred Swaine, Smith, Sidney, ed., revised by Cook, W.G.H. & Stewart, C.P., *Taylor's Principles and Practice of Medical Jurisprudence*, 10th ed. Vols. 1 & 2, J & A Churchill, London, 1948.

Timbers, Frances, 'Witches' Sect or Prayer Meeting?: Matthew Hopkins revisited', *Women's History Review*, Vol. 17(1), pp. 21–37.

Treasury Solicitor and HM Procurator General: Law Officers' and Counsel's Opinions, Suspected poisoning of Richard Chesham by his wife Sarah Chesham, 21 August 1850, The National Archives, reference: TS 25/513.

Unknown, 'The Execution of Sarah Chesham', Hodges, London, 1851, the British Library, 74/1888.c.3.

Unknown, *The New International Encyclopedia*, 1905, sourced from Wikimedia Commons.

Watson, Katherine, *Poisoned Lives: English Poisoners and their Victims*, Hambledon & London, London, 2004.

Wiener, Martin J., 'Judges v Jurors: Courtroom tensions in murder trials and the law of criminal responsibility in nineteenth-century England', *Law and History Review*, Vol. 17 (3), 1999, pp. 467–506.

References

Newspapers:
CC: *Chelmsford Chronicle*
ES: *Essex Standard*
IJ: *Ipswich Journal*
TT: *The Times*

Archives:
ERO: Essex Record Office
LMA: London Metropolitan Archives
TNA: The National Archives

Introduction
Satire on poison availability:
Punch, Vol. 17, 1849.

Food colouring death:
Northampton Mercury, 22 July 1848.

Arsenic:
Taylor, Alfred Swaine, Smith, Sidney, ed., Revised by Cook, W.G.H. & Stewart, C.P., *Taylor's Principles and Practice of Medical Jurisprudence*, 10th ed., J & A Churchill, London, 1948. Vol. 2, p. 121.
Developing Treatments: Poisons as Treatments, Museum of the Royal Pharmaceutical Society, London, 2006.
Letheby, H., 'On the Probability of Confounding Cases of Arsenical Poisoning with those of Cholera', *Pharmaceutical Journal*, Vol. 8, 1848–1849, pp. 237–40.
Emsley, John, *Elements of Murder: A History of Poison*, Oxford University Press, 2005 pp. 105–106, 110–11, 122, 150–1.

Surgeons in Essex:
Census of Great Britain, 1841, *Abstract of the answers and returns.*

Madam Lafarge:
Flanders, Judith, *The Invention of Murder: How the Victorians Revelled in Death and Detection and Created Modern Crime*, HarperPress, London, 2011, p. 253.

Spousal murder:
Robb, George, 'Circe in crinoline: domestic poisonings in Victorian England', *Journal of Family History*, 22(2), April 1997, pp.176, 179.

Chapter 1
Conditions of the Essex poor:
Peacock, A.J., 'Village radicalism in East Anglia, 1800–1850', in *Rural discontent in nineteenth-century Britain* by J.P.D. Dunbabin, Faber & Faber, London, 1974. p. 46.
TT, 20 June 1844.
CC, 4 January 1844.

Chesham family:
Clavering parish registers: ERO D/P 333/1/3, D/P 333/1/6, D/P 333/1/7, D/P 333/1/8.
Census of Great Britain, 1841, *Abstract of the answers and returns*. Notes by the enumerators state that hundreds of men were haymaking away from home, sleeping in barns.

The Happisburgh poisonings:
TT, 19 & 20 May 1846.
Letter to *Norfolk News*, 18 July 1846, by William Clowes, a local doctor involved in the cases who wrote to his local paper to correct errors printed in newspapers countrywide.

The inquests:
CC, 21 & 28 August; 11 & 25 September; 2, 16 & 30 October; 6 November 1846.
ES, 21 & 28 August; 16 October 1846.
TT, 20 & 21 August 1846.
London Standard, 26 August 1846.

The trials:
ES, 5 & 12 March 1847.
TT, 12 March 1847.

Seventeenth-century witchcraft beliefs:
See Gaskill, Malcolm, *Witchfinders: A Seventeenth-Century English Tragedy*, John Murray, London, 2006.
Timbers, Frances, 'Witches' Sect or Prayer Meeting?: Matthew Hopkins revisited', *Women's History Review*, Vol. 17(1), pp.21–37.

Nineteenth-century police:
Emsley, Clive, *The English Police: a political and social history*, 2nd ed., Longman, London, 1996, especially pp. 11, 25, 26, 51.

On inquests:
Ballantine, Serjeant (William), *Some Experiences of a Barrister's Life*, 8th ed., Richard Bentley, London, 1883, p. 234.

Nineteenth-century newspapers and their readers:
Brown, Lucy, *Victorian news and newspapers*, Clarendon Press, Oxford, 1985. pp. 18–21.
Barker, Hannah, *Newspapers, politics and English society, 1695–1855*, Pearson, Harlow, 2000, pp. 53–8.

Newport's railway opens:
CC, 1 August 1845.

Manuden burial register:
ERO D/P 272/1/11.

Lucretia reviews and response:
Medical Gazette, 5 February 1847, p. 243.
TT, 17 December 1846.
Bulwer-Lytton, Edward, *A Word to the Public*, Leipzig: Tauchnitz, 1847, p.29.
ES, 12 February 1847.

Thomas Newport's arrest:
CC, 22 & 29 January 1847.
ES, 29 January 1847.

On nineteenth-century trials:
Wiener, Martin J., 'Judges v Jurors: Courtroom tensions in murder trials and the law of criminal responsibility in nineteenth-century England', *Law and History Review*, Vol. 17 (3), 1999, pp.473, 474.
Ballantine, *ibid*, p. 263.

On Denman and Jones:
The New International Encyclopedia, 1905.
Bury & Norwich Post, 21 July 1852.

Brookes's letter:
TT, 18 March 1847.

Marriage of David Gray and Sarah Bright:
Little Dunmow marriage register: ERO D/P 95/1/12.

Catherine Foster:
Hardy, Sheila, *Arsenic in the Dumplings: A Casebook of Historic Poisonings in Suffolk*, History Press, Stroud, 2010, pp.41–53.
Bury & Norwich Post, 27 March 1847.

Cost of Sarah Chesham's trials:
CC, 2 July 1847.

Thomas Newport's trial:
ES, 16 July 1847.

Marriage of Charles Parker and Lydia Taylor:
Manuden marriage register: ERO D/P 272/1/10.

On Emma Elizabeth Hume:
ES, 30 April; 16 July 1847.
Tollesbury parish registers: ERO D/P 283/1/12, ERO ref D/P 283/1/5.
Petition against her sentence: TNA HO18/204.
Transportation: www.convictrecords.com.au; Microfilm Roll 92, Class and Piece Number HO11/15, p. 252.

Chapter 2
Inspector Raison:
Cases around the Tendring & Lexden Hundreds: *ES*, 1 November 1844; *ES*, 13 November 1846; *ES*, 8 October 1847.
Joins the Essex Constabulary, promotion to inspector, dismissal: ERO J/P 2/1.
Dismissal and reinstatement: Clark, Roy, *History Notebook Number 11: The Harwich Death Club*, Essex Police Museum, Chelsmford, unknown year, www.essex.police. uk/museum.

Mary May's parentage:
Wix marriage register: ERO D/P 172/1/3A.
Evidence of Mary Feint on William Constable's parentage: TNA HO 18/239.
The marriage certificate of Mary May, on marrying her second husband, gives her father's name as James Ainger, so the 1808 marriage of James Angier and Mary Constable in Wix must be that of Mary's parents. To avoid confusion, the spelling 'Angier' is used throughout.

The family of William Constable, alias Spratty Watts:
Great Oakley and Wix parish registers, ERO D/P 47/1/9, D/P 47/1/11, D/P 172/1/7, D/P 172/1/8.

Mary May's husband and children:
Ramsey parish registers: ERO D/P 7/1/5, D/P 7/1/6, D/P 7/1/7.
ES, 21 December 1849 (Rev Wilkins's letter about Mary May's origins).
James Everett and Mary Angier married in Ramsey on 7 September 1825. Their six children baptised in that village were: Caroline (baptised 25 June 1826, buried 22 May 1827, aged 11 months), James (born 28 October 1828, baptised privately 6 December 1828, buried 20 October 1830), Eliza (baptised 13 December 1831. Appears on 1841 census in Wix. Buried there 2 October 1841, aged 10), Alfred (baptised 17 March 1836, buried 4 April 1836, aged 6 weeks), William (baptised 24 January 1839), Ellen (baptised 21 June 1840, buried 25 June 1840, an infant). James Everett was buried in Ramsey on 23 September 1840, aged 36.
Jemima May appears once in the GRO index of registered births for 1845, and twice in the baptism register. The first time seems to have been a private baptism and the second was when she was 'received into the church' a year later. Her brother William is mysterious: he appears once, at his baptism, and possibly in the index of births for 1847. It has not been possible to trace him further with any certainty. Mary's children are never referred to by name in any newspaper reports, except when William Everett gave evidence in court.

William Constable, alias Spratty Watts, alias William Watts, on trial:
ES, 14 April 1848.

Wix National School:
Minutes of the Committee of Council on education: with appendices, 1847–1848, Vol. 1. W. Clowes, London, 1848.

Burial clubs:
Bowley's tables of wages show that an Essex agricultural labourer could earn on average 8s a week in 1850. This would yield just under £21 a year. Bowley, A.L., 'The Statistics of Wages in the United Kingdom during the Last Hundred Years, part 1', *Journal of the Royal Statistical Society,* Vol. 61(4), 1898, p.704.
Morning Chronicle, 2 January 1850
Hurren, Elizabeth, 'Patients' rights: from Alder Hey to the Nuremberg Code', 6 May 2002, in *History & Policy,* retrieved 6 June 2015, www.historyandpolicy.org.
TT, 11 January 1845; 13 August & 14 October 1846.
Chadwick, Edwin, *Report on the sanitary condition of the labouring population of Great Britain: a supplementary report on the results of a special inquiry into the practice of interment in towns made at the request of Her Majesty's Principal Secretary of State for the Home Department,* W. Clowes, London, 1843. pp. 63–5.

Nagy, Victoria M., 'Narratives in the courtroom: Female poisoners in mid-nineteenth-century England', *European Journal of Criminology*, Vol 11(2), 2014, p. 221.

White Hart public house:
www.pubshistory.com.

The weather:
CC, 16 June 1848.

Inquest:
ES, 7 & 14 July 1848.
CC, 14 July 1848.
Mary May identified Butler's Rat Poison at the inquest as being what she had bought, but this was not mentioned in reports of the inquest, and appears in reports of the trial.

Trial:
TNA ref: HO 18/239.
CC, 28 July 1848.
TT, 25 July 1848.
ES, 28 July 1848 (trial); 21 December 1849 (fees for Mary May's defence counsel).
Charles Tweed said Mary approached him on 28 June, and Inspector Raison said he approached Mary on 29 June. These dates don't quite fit – either there was a mistake in the newspaper report, or Mary knew before Inspector Raison told her that an inquest was to take place, which might explain why she asked Tweed to spread lies for her.

Reverend Wilkins:
Bell's Weekly Messenger, 31 July 1848 (letter to *Essex Herald* about potato blight, quoted in *Bell's*).
ES, 16 March 1877 (obituary).

Wix burial register:
ERO ref: D/P 172/1/8.

Mortality rates:
Daunton, Martin, 'Society and economic life', in Matthew, Colin, ed., *The Nineteenth Century. The British Isles: 1815–1901*. Oxford University Press, 2000, p.63.

Execution:
CC, 4, 11 & 18 August; 3 November 1848.
ES, 4 & 18 August 1848.
TT, 15 August 1848.
The Newgate Calendar, Vol. 4, p.260 (on Elizabeth Larghan).
TNA ref: HO 18/239 (Pollock's letter).
Rowley, Sheila V., *Little Baddow: The history of an Essex village, part three*, Little Baddow, 1979, p. 55, retrieved from www.mel-thompson.co.uk (William Calcraft).
Mayhew, Henry, *London Labour and the London Poor*, Vol. 1: The London Street Folk, *Morning Chronicle*, London, 1851, pp. 282–3, 307.

Chapter 3
Hannah Southgate's family:
Manningtree Wesleyan Methodist church baptisms TNA ref: RG 4/795.
Wix parish registers ERO refs: D/P 172/1/7, D/P 172/1/8.
Tendring parish registers: D/P 353/1/5, D/P 353/1/7, D/P 353/1/11.
Thomas Ham's profession can be seen on his children's baptism records and on the census.
Will of John Ham, late of Bradfield, now of Wix, yeoman, 1825. ERO ref: D/ACW 41/2/25.
ES, 7 April 1832 (suicide of Thomas Ham's brother).

Superstitions surrounding death:
Bronte, Emily, *Wuthering Heights*, Puffin (Penguin), London, 1994, p. 151.
Letter by W.F. Herbert to *The Spectator*, 29 June 1901.

The inquest:
CC, 25 August; 1 & 8 September 1848.
ES, 1 September 1848.
TT, 29 August; 1 & 20 September 1848.

The trial:
CC, 9 March 1849.
ES, 9 March 1849.
IJ, 10 March 1849.
TT, 10 March 1849.
'Blast you', being shorthand for 'blast you to hell', was considered too strong to print in full at the time. It is rendered 'b—t' in the newspaper report.
Ballantine, Serjeant (William), *Some Experiences of a Barrister's Life*, 8th ed., Richard Bentley, London, 1883, pp. 93, 95, 108–109, 146, 204-208, 216.
Lewis, J R., *The Victorian Bar*, Robert Hale, London, 1982, p.63 (on Ballantine).

Marriage statistics:
Phegley, Jennifer, *Courtship and Marriage in Victorian England*, Praeger, Santa Barbara, 2012, pp. 157–8.

Charlotte Elvish's family:
CC, 7 April 1843 (potato theft).
Fingringhoe baptisms ERO D/P 369/1/2.
Will of Thomas Jaggard of Fingringhoe, farmer, 1812, ERO D/ABW 199/2/52.
Will of Thomas Jaggard of Wix, yeoman, 1852 ERO D/ACW 45/1/27.
Wivenhoe parish registers: ERO D/P 277/1/6, D/P 277/1/10.
Thorpe-le-Soken marriage register ERO D/P 8/1/9.

European revolution and its effect on Britain:
Alpert, Michael, *London 1849: A Victorian Murder Story*, Pearson, Harlow, 2004, pp.166, 169.
Dasent, Arthur Irwin, *John Thadeus Delane, editor of The Times. His Life & Correspondence*, Vol. 1, John Murray, London, 1908, p. 76.

Sensational reports:
ES, 6 October 1848.
TT, 14 & 20 September 1848.
The Observer, 18 September 1848.
Ramsey burial register ERO D/P 7/1/6.
Great Holland registers ERO D/P 396/1/5, D/P 396/1/8.

Nathaniel Button inquest:
TT, 21, 22 & 26 September 1848; 6 September 1848. Letter from William Payne.
Dasent, *ibid*, p.27.
CC, 6 October 1848.

The Times's campaign against poison sales:
TT, 7 August; 20 October 1848; 24 October 1848. Letter from T G Maggs.

Mary Ann Geering:
Watson, Katherine, *Poisoned Lives: English Poisoners and their Victims*, Hambledon & London, London, 2004, pp. 87–8.

Maria Manning:
See Borowitz, Albert, *The Bermondsey Horror*, Robson Books, London, 1988.
Ballantine, *ibid*, p.156.
Flanders, *ibid*, pp. 170–2.

John Sadler trial:

Old Bailey Proceedings Online (www.oldbaileyonline.org, version 7.2, 31 August
2015), April 1850, trial of JOHN SADLER (t18500408-694) and 5 July 2015),
May 1850, trial of JOHN SADLER (t18500506-990).

Ballantine, *ibid*, p.110.

London Daily News, 10 April 1850.

'Lucky Hannah Southgate':

CC, 1 June 1849.

ES, 16 August 1854.

Chapter 4

Inquest & magistrates' investigation:

CC, 24 May; 27 September 1850.

ES, 14 June; 27 September 1850.

Rai, S. and Thomas, W.M., 'Diagnosis of abdominal tuberculosis: the importance
of laparoscopy', in *J R Soc Med.*, Dec 2003; 96(12): 586–8.

Treasury Solicitor and HM Procurator General: Law Officers' and Counsel's
Opinions. Suspected poisoning of Richard Chesham by his wife Sarah Chesham.
21 August 1850, TNA TS 25/513.

The weather:

ES & *CC*, 31 May 1850.

Professor Taylor's other cases & the police:

Flanders, *ibid*, pp.259–66.

Parry, Leonard A., ed., *Trial of Dr Smethurst (Notable British Trials)*, William
Hodge, Edinburgh & London, 1931, pp. 84–6.

Ballantine, *ibid*, pp. 212–17.

Parry, *ibid*, pp. 86–7.

Hardy, *ibid*, pp. 26–31.

See Summerscale, Kate, *The Suspicions of Mr Whicher: or The Murder at Road Hill
House*, Bloomsbury, London, 2008.

Doddinghurst murder:

ES, 18 October 1850.

Charles Chadwick Jones:

TT, 22 February 1850.

Bell's Life in London, 11 July 1852.

Trial:
CC, 7 & 14 March 1851.
ES, 28 February; 7 March 1851.
TT, 7, 8 & 12 March 1851.

Sale of Arsenic Regulation Bill:
HL Hansard, Sale of Arsenic Regulation Bill: 13, 14 & 24 March 1851.
Mill, John Stuart, *The Collected Works of John Stuart Mill, Volume XIV: The Later Letters of John Stuart Mill, 1849–1873 part I*, eds. ,www.oll.libertyfund.org, 5 May 1851.

Execution:
CC, 28 March 1851.
ES, 14, 21 & 28 March; 4 April 1851.
Royal Cornwall Gazette, 28 March 1851.
TT, 26 March 1851.
Mayhew, *ibid*, p. 225.
Unknown, 'The Execution of Sarah Chesham', Hodges, London, 1851.
British Geological Survey, arsenical analysis of Cornish water sources, www.bgs.ac.uk/research/highlights/2013/arsenicSW.html.

Execution aftermath:
ES, 4 & 18 April 1851.
Clavering burial register: ERO D/P 333/1/7.

Chapter 5
Reverend Wilkins:
ES, 30 November; 7 & 21 December 1849.
ES, 8 & 27 Aug 1856.

Robert May's suicide:
ES, 13 June 1851.
CC, 13 June 1851.
Wix burial and baptism registers: ERO D/P 172/1/7, D/P 172/1/8.

Inspector Samuel Raison:
ES, 3 January 1851; 4 June 1852.
CC, 17 January 1851.

The Cheshams:
Huddersfield Chronicle, 2 August 1851.
Emigration to Australia: www.records.nsw.gov.au.

Clavering crimes and memories of Sarah Chesham:
ES, 22 January 1862; 2 May 1903.
CC, 5 June 1903; 6 March 1908; 14 Sep 1928.

Emma Elizabeth Hume:
Hobart Town Daily Mercury, 31 Mar 1859.
Marriage and death information: www.linc.tas.gov.au.

Hannah Southgate:
Essex Newsman, 25 Oct 1884.
ES, 14 Jan 1893.
Banstead Asylum records LMA ref: H22/BAN/B/01/010, LMA ref: H22/BAN/B/07/16.
Johansson, L. et al, 'Common psychosocial stressors in middle-aged women related to longstanding distress and increased risk of Alzheimer's disease: a 38-year longitudinal population study', *BMJ Open*, 2013.

Index